Welcome

It is always our great pleasure to welcome all visitors to Pembrokeshire, and we hope that you can use our guide to maximi… embrokeshire is a county steeped in history, myth… centuries. The evidence of the sweeping … re are evident everywhere you look, from … Age Forts and Bronze Age burial chambe… serve a very practical purpose during you… guides. After your stay you will be able to … through all the background information abo… that you visited. We genuinely hope that you enjoy your visit to our beautiful county and that you can use our guide to get the most out of your holiday.

Please enjoy your stay.

Pembrokeshire places
FINDING US

Ferry to Rosslare
CARDIGAN
Newcastle Emlyn
Fishguard
Newport
Dinas Head
Strumble Head
Newport Bay
Fishguard Bay
MYNYDD PRESELI
PEMBROKESHIRE COAST NATIONAL PARK
St Davids
Ramsey Island
ST BRIDES BAY
HAVERFORDWEST
Narberth
Whitland
Milford Haven
Pembroke Dock
Pembroke
Tenby
Caldey Island
CARMARTHEN BAY
Skomer Island
Skokholm Island
Saundersfoot Bay
Saundersfoot
Penally
Manorbier
Stackpole
St Govan's Head
Saddle Head
Linney Head
Angle
Dale
Solva
Newgale
Broad Haven
Little Haven
Crymych
Cilgerran
St Dogmaels
Abereiddy
Porthgain
Trevine
Goodwick
Lower Town
Mathry
Letterston
Neyland
Kilgetty
Amroth
Pendine
Clunderwen
Llanddewi Velfrey
Templeton
Carew
Lamphey
Freshwater East
Broad Haven
Bosherston
St Florence
Lydstep
Jameston
Caldey Sound
St Margaret's Island
Monkstone Point
Wiseman's Bridge
1
2
3
4
5
7
8
9
10
11
12
13
14
15
17
18
19
23
24
25
27
28
29
30
31
32
33
34
35
38
39
40
41
42
43
44
45
47
48
49
50
51
52
53
54
55
57
58
59

CONTENTS

BEACH GUIDE

Pembrokeshire is truly blessed with some of the most stunning beaches in the country. Offering delights from the ever popular beaches at Saundersfoot and Tenby to the secluded magic of sandy stretches of Barafundle and Whitesands. If you are more of an active persuasion, please see our activities section for the best beaches for water based sports.

Life's a Beach

Beach	Description	Water Quality	Green Coast Award	Blue Flag Beach (2014)	Seaside Award Beach	Toilets (Disabled)	Phone/or Emergency Phone	Lifeguard/Beach Attendant	First Aid	Coastal Bus Service	Car Park	Slipway or Launching	Mooring	Harbour	Bathing	Sea Angling	Sub Aqua	Canoeing/Kayaking	Surfing	Sea Rowing	Sailing	Wind Surf	Water Ski	Cafe	Powerboat	Beware Currents	Dog Restriction	Pontoon	No Dog Fouling
ST. DOGMAELS	M F E	NT				WC (D)	•			B		•	•					•		•	•					!			NF
POPPIT	S D	E			*	WC (D)	•	•	+	B	P				•			•	•			•		•		!	•		NF
CEIBWR	R S	NT														•	•	•											NF
NEWPORT SANDS	S D	E			*	WC (D)	•	•	+	B	P	•			•	•	•	•		•	•	•		•					NF
NEWPORT PARROG	E S R	NT				WC (D)	•			B	P	•	•			•		•		•	•	•			•	!			NF
CWM-YR-EGLWYS	S ST RP	E			*	WC (D)					P	•	•		•	•	•	•			•	•							NF
PWLL GWAELOD	S SH	NT				WC (D)	•			B	P	•			•	•	•	•			•								NF
LOWER FISHGUARD	H	NT				WC	•			B	P	•	•	•		•	•	•		•	•				•				NF
GOODWICK SANDS	S ST	E			*	WC (D)	•			B	P	•			•	•		•			•	•	•	•					NF
ABERBACH (ST. NICHOLAS)	P S C	NT								B						•										!			NF
ABERMAWR	P S R	E								B					•	•			•							!			NF
ABERCASTLE	R C SH	NT				WC	•			B		•	•			•	•	•			•								NF
ABERFELIN/TREFIN	SH R C	NT				WC (D)				B						•	•	•											NF
PORTHGAIN	H	NT				WC (D)	•			B	P	•	•	•		•	•	•											NF
TRAETHLLYFN	S R C RP	NT																								!			NF
ABEREIDDY	S R C RP	E			*	WC	•			B	P				•	•	•	•	•							!			NF
PORTHMELGEN	C R S	NT														•										!			NF
WHITESANDS	S ST R	E		✓	*	WC (D)	•	•	+	B	P	•			•	•	•	•	•			•		•		!	•	X	NF
PORTHSELAU	R S C	E													•											!			NF
PORTHCLAIS	H	NT				WC (D)	•			B	P	•	•	•		•	•	•			•								NF
CAERFAI	S C R	E	●		*					B	P				•	•										!			NF
SOLVA	H	NT				WC (D)	•			B	P	•	•	•		•	•	•		•	•			•					NF
NEWGALE	P S C ST	E		✓	*	WC (D)	•	•	+	B	P				•	•		•	•			•		•		!	•	X	NF
NOLTON HAVEN	C S ST R	G				WC (D)	•			B	P	•			•	•	•	•			•					!			NF
DRUIDSTON	C S P ST	E	●							B					•	•										!			NF
BROAD HAVEN	S P ST R	E		✓	*	WC (D)	•	•	+	B	P	•			•	•	•	•	•	•	•	•		•			•		NF
LITTLE HAVEN	S ST R	E			*	WC (D)	•			B	P	•			•	•	•	•		•	•	•	•	•					NF
ST. BRIDES HAVEN	R S ST	E			*	WC	•			B	P				•	•	•	•								!			NF
MARTINS HAVEN	R P	E	●		*	WC	•			B	P	•			•	•	•	•								!			NF
MARLOES SANDS	S C R	E	●		*	WC (D)	•			B	P				•	•										!			NF
WEST DALE	S C R	E														•			•							!			NF
DALE	P S R ST	E		✓	*	WC (D)	•		+	B	P	•	•		•	•	•	•			•	•	•	•			•	X	NF
LINDSWAY BAY	SR	NT														•										!			NF
SANDY HAVEN	C R S	G			*						P	•			•	•		•			•					!			NF
GELLISWICK	S R	G			*	WC	•				P	•			•	•		•			•	•			•				NF
LLANSTADWELL	S E	NT				WC	•			B	P	•	•					•										X	NF
NEYLAND	SH MF	NT				WC	•			B	P	•	•	•		•	•	•		•	•	•	•		•	!		X	NF
BURTON	E	NT				WC (D)	•			B	P	•	•			•		•			•	•	•		•	!		X	NF
LLANGWM/BLACKTAR	E SH	NT				WC	•			B	P	•	•			•		•		•	•	•	•		•				NF
LAWRENNY	E SH MF	NT				WC	•				P	•	•	•				•			•		•		•				NF
EAST LLANION	E	E									P	•	•					•			•			•	•				NF
ANGLE BAY	E MF	NT								B		•	•					•			•								NF
WEST ANGLE BAY	R S	G	●		*	WC	•			B	P				•	•		•			•	•		•		!			NF
FRESHWATER WEST	S R ST D	E				WC (D)	•	•	+	B	P			BEWARE OF STRONG RIP CURRENTS												!			NF
BROAD HAVEN SOUTH	S D ST	E	●		*	WC (D)	•			B	P				•	•		•	•							!			NF
BARAFUNDLE BAY	S D ST	E	●		*					B					•														NF
STACKPOLE QUAY	H	NT				WC (D)	•			B	P			•		•		•						•					NF
FRESHWATER EAST	S D ST	E	●		*	WC (D)	•			B	P	•	•		•	•		•	•		•	•	•	•	•				NF
MANORBIER	S D ST	E	●		*	WC (D)	•			B	P				•	•		•	•					•		!			NF
LYDSTEP HAVEN	S SH	E		✓	*	WC (D)	•		+	B	P	•	•		•	•	•	•			•	•	•	•	•		•	X	NF
PENALLY	S D	E	●		*	WC (D)	•			B	P				•	•													NF
PRIORY BAY CALDEY	S	E	●			WC	•		+						•	•		•						•					NF
TENBY SOUTH	S D	E		✓	*	WC (D)	•	•	+	B	P				•	•		•	•			•		•			•	X	NF
TENBY CASTLE	S	E		✓	*	WC (D)	•	•	+	B					•	•	•	•						•	•	!	•	X	NF
TENBY HARBOUR	H	NT				WC (D)	•		+		P	•	•	•	•	•		•		•				•	•		•	X	NF
TENBY NORTH	S	E		✓	*	WC (D)	•	•	+	B	P				•	•		•			•		•	•	•		•	X	NF
MONKSTONE	S R	E														•													NF
GLEN BEACH	S R	G	●		*	WC	•		+	B	P				•	•		•											NF
SAUNDERSFOOT	S H	E		✓	*	WC (D)	•	•	+	B	P	•	•	•	•	•	•	•			•	•	•	•	•		•		NF
COPPET HALL	S R	E		✓	*	WC (D)	•			B	P				•	•		•			•			•			•		NF
WISEMANS BRIDGE	S R	G			*	WC (D)	•			B	P				•	•													NF
AMROTH	S R	E		✓	*	WC (D)	•	•	+	B	P				•	•		•			•		•	•	•		•	X	NF

Beach Description Key

S SAND BEACH	P PEBBLE BEACH	ST STREAM	R ROCKY	RP ROCK POOLS	E ESTUARY
D SAND DUNES	C CLIFFS	SH SHINGLE	MF MUD FLATS	H HARBOUR	X PONTOON

Water Quality gradings: **EXCELLENT** = complies with the E.C. Excellent standard. **GOOD** = complies with the sufficent standard. Beaches that are not tested are generally smaller, adjacent to tested beaches or in isolated locations.

Blue Flags are the European standard for quality beaches with excellent water quality and a good range of facilities such as toilets.

Seaside awards are a U.K. only scheme for beaches with at least good water quality but they may not achieve all criteria needed for a Blue Flag award.

Green Coast awards are for isolated rural beaches with excellent water quality but few or no facilities

Lifeboats

Look out for these flags, they mark bathing areas patrolled by life guards.

Two black & white flags mark non swimming areas zoned mainly for surfing, windsurfing or a motorised craft beach access point.

Take note of this flag, it indicates dangerous conditions, DO NOT GO SWIMMING when it's flying.

All awards shown have been applied for the 2015 season

WATER QUALITY:
E = EXCELLENT G = GOOD
NT = NOT TESTED

Lifeguards & Beach attendants on duty from the last week in June to the first weekend in September 10am tom 6pm daily

Please take note of the flags (ask the lifeguards if you're in doubt) and ensure that everyone has a happy - and safe - day at the beach!

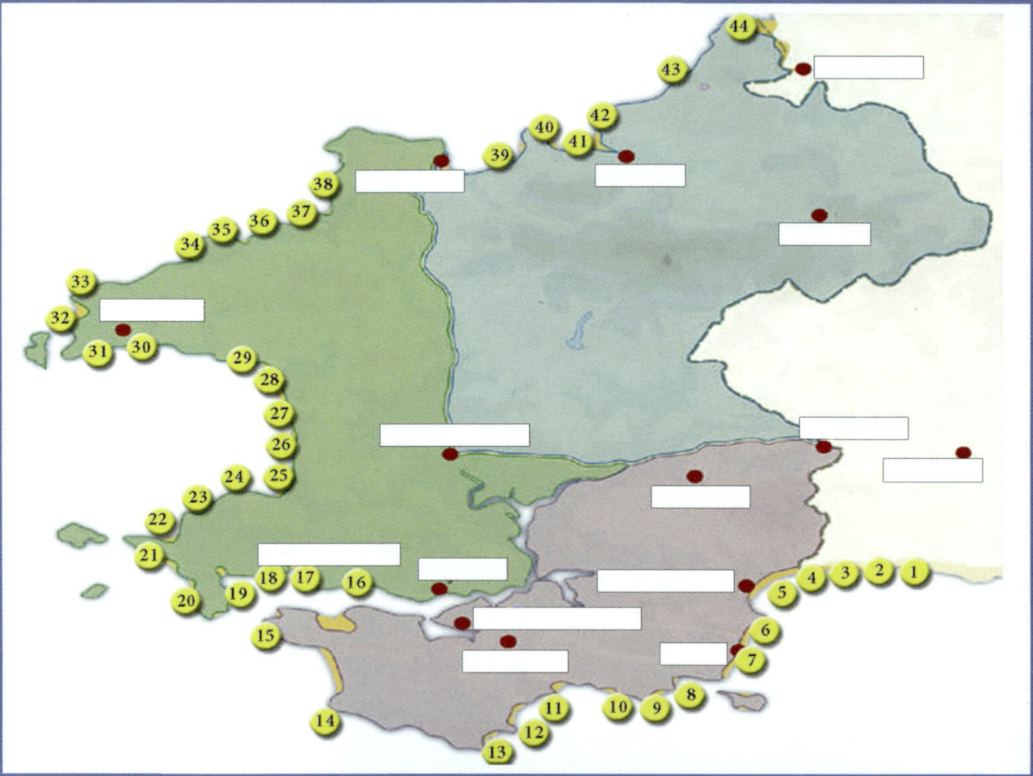

SOUTH COAST

It is no surprise that many visitors to Pembrokeshire come here first and foremost for the county's magnificent sandy beaches. Our counties beaches are regular award winners throughout the years, please check page 6 of this guide for this year's up to date information. So whether you are a sun worshipper, watersports fanatic, boat owner or you simply love the seaside, Pembrokeshire is an idyllic place to enjoy the great beach holiday.

AMROTH (1)

Amroth is a charming coastal village where time seems to have stood still. The beach is punctuated by a series of groynes that help protect the village from winter storms and rough seas. The Eastern end marks the start of the renowned 186 mile Pembrokeshire Coastal Path. Parking is good along the seafront and in the village.

Amroth

Coppet Hall

WISEMANS BRIDGE (2)

The beach's claim to fame is that it was used in 1944 for rehearsals of the D Day landings under the watchful eye of Sir Winston Churchill himself. The beach is sandy and it's possible to walk to neighbouring Saundersfoot at low tide. Parking is limited.

COPPET HALL (3)

Coppet Hall is a popular beach which has extensive parking facilities. It also affords access to Saundersfoot village.

SAUNDERSFOOT (4)

Saundersfoot is one of the area's most popular resorts and it's easy to see why. There is everything for the family including a superb beach and a range of shops, cafes and restaurants. There is also a picturesque harbour plus extensive parking facilities.

MONKSTONE (5)

Monkstone (Saundersfoot) is unsuitable for families as access is down very steep steps. Those hardy enough to make the journey will find a beautiful stretch of sand but no facilities. Entry to the beach is through Trevayne Farm off the B4316 near New Hedges. There is a small charge for parking.

TENBY NORTH (6)

Tenby is one of the most popular seaside resorts in Wales. A medieval walled town with narrow streets, it stands on a rocky headland which divides its two main beaches. The award winning North Beach has first class facilities together with a picture postcard harbour and sandy beach. Because of the town's narrow streets, visitors are advised to park in one of the large car parks outside the town walls, all of which are within walking distance of the beaches.

TENBY SOUTH (7)

Tenby's South Beach offers a large expanse of fine sand. A firm favourite with people holidaying at the nearby Kiln Park Holiday Village. The beach, which is backed by cliffs on which the town stands, offers unlimited views of Caldey Island which is inhabited by monks. Facilities are excellent.

Tenby

Saundersfoot

Tenby

LYDSTEP HAVEN (8)

Lydstep Haven is a privately owned beautiful sheltered bay for which there is an admission charge. Characterised at either end by wooded cliffs, Lydstep boasts a slipway to cater for the many boats and pleasure crafts using the bay. One of the area's main features is the Smugglers Cave, which can be explored even at high tide.

SKRINKLE HAVEN (9)

Skrinkle Haven is an absolute gem of a beach sheltered by tall cliffs. However, there is no access to the public. There is a car park above the beach but no other facilities.

MANORBIER (10)

Manorbier is very popular with surfers. Overlooked by a medieval castle and the 12th Century church of St James, the beach is the home to a stone cromlech known as the King's Quoit. The sandy beach is served by a large car park, together with parking areas on the road above the beach.

FRESHWATER EAST (11)

Freshwater East is a wide, sweeping crescent of sand and shingle backed by dunes and grassy headlands. Popular with boat owners, divers, fishermen and surfers.

Freshwater West

BARAFUNDLE (12)

Barafundle is surely one of Pembrokeshire's most beautiful beaches, it is however only accessible from the coastal path. Owned by the National Trust, the nearest parking is at Stackpole Quay about half a mile away. Due to its remote location the beach itself has no amenities, but there is a tearoom at Stackpole Quay.

BROAD HAVEN SOUTH (13)

Broad Haven South is a superb sheltered beach popular with sun worshipers. Another of the National Trust owned beaches, it offers excellent parking for both those visiting the beach or those using it as a gateway to the area's many fine walks.

FRESHWATER WEST (14)

Freshwater West is a haven for surfers. They are drawn to the area by the big Atlantic rollers so it seems only natural that the beach has been used for the Welsh National Surfing Championships. However, it can be dangerous to swimmers because of strong rip currents and hazardous quicksands so families with small children should be on their guard.

Freshwater East

Barafundle

Dale

WEST COAST

WEST ANGLE BAY (15)

West Angle Bay is another beautiful location, very popular with visitors and local inhabitants alike. Low tides reveal rock pools, which youngsters can explore. The beach houses the remains of an old lime kiln now partly overgrown. There are excellent walks along the cliffs offering spectacular views. Parking and other facilities are good.

GELLISWICK (16)

Gelliswick is the headquarters of the Pembrokeshire Yacht Club and offers an excellent slipway for boats. A large sand and shingle beach, facilities include toilets, free parking and the nearby shops of Milford Haven.

SANDY HAVEN (17)

Sandy Haven beach is sandwiched between the village of Sandy Haven and Herbrandston. Just below Herbrandston lies a sandy beach, which at low tide offers superb views of the estuary. Unsuitable for swimming however, because of unpredictable estuary currents. Parking on both sides of the western and eastern sides of the estuary are limited.

LINDSWAY BAY (18)

Lindsway Bay is not suitable for bathing, but because of its position to the Milford Haven Waterway, it makes an ideal place for walking, bird watching and collecting shellfish. Enveloped by cliffs and large rocks, it also offers good views of St. Ann's Head from both the beach and the cliff top. South of the bay is Great Castle Head, the site of an Iron Age Fort. The beach is devoid of amenities and parking is a quarter of a mile away.

DALE (19)

If it's watersports you're interested in then this is the place to be. Dale is home to yachting, windsurfing and a watersports centre. It is also attractive to the sub-aqua
fraternity because of its wreck sites. Facilities in the attractive village overlooking the sea are good and there is a large carpark opposite the shingle beach.

WEST DALE (20)

West Dale is a stunning secluded cove, but its sand and shingle beach can be dangerous to swimmers because of undertows and unpredictable currents and hidden rocks. Access is via road or footpath through Dale, but parking is limited and there are no amenities.

West Angle Bay

Angle

Dale

MARLOES (21)

Marloes sands is a magnificent beach, characterised by outcrops of rocks and a large crescent of golden sand at low tide, which was inhabited from prehistoric to medieval times and which still bears the remains of 5th century huts. Another feature are the Three Chimneys - horizontal beds of rock, more than 400 million years old. The National Trust has a car park half a mile from the beach, but the nearest facilities are about a mile away in the village of Marloes.

MARTINS HAVEN (22)

Martins Haven is a small north facing cove with a pebble beach. Boat trips operate from here to the Skomer Nature Reserve. Facilities include toilets and parking.

MUSSELWICK (23)

Musselwick Sands is a fine sandy beach that is only exposed at low tide. Access is difficult and visitors need to be aware that the tide could cut them off. There are no amenities and parking at the start of the long footpath to the beach is limited.

ST. BRIDES HAVEN (24)

St. Bride's Haven is a sheltered cove with a beach of shingle, pebbles and rock pools, enhanced at low tide by sand. Interesting features near the beach include an early Christian Cemetery with stone lined graves and the remains of an old limekiln. There is limited parking near the church.

LITTLE HAVEN (25)

Little Haven is a small sandy cove with a slipway for small boats, including the local inshore rescue boat. There is a pay and display car park close to the beach and numerous facilities including pubs offering food and drink and other useful shops.

BROAD HAVEN WEST (26)

Broad Haven (west) is a large magnificent expanse of sand, which runs the entire length of Broad Haven village. It is a favourite with bathers and water-sport enthusiasts, and also has a great deal to interest geologists with an abundance of different rock formations. The village offers good facilities and a choice of car parks.

Little Haven

Broad Haven

Marloes

Broad Haven

WEST COAST

Newgale

DRUIDSTON HAVEN (27)

Druidston Haven, whilst being a long sandy beach, is not suitable for bathers because of strong currents. Enclosed on three sides by steep cliffs, access to the beach is by two footpaths. However, there is only limited parking on the roadside and there are no amenities.

NOLTON HAVEN (28)

Nolton Haven is a beach of sand and shingle with cliffs on either side. A red flag flying warns of danger to swimmers. There is a National Trust car park above the beach.

NEWGALE SANDS (29)

Newgale Sands is another broad expanse of sand exposed to the Atlantic gales, which acts as a magnet to surfers and other watersports enthusiasts. During summer lifeguards designate areas for swimmers and patrol this excellent beach. There is a shop, two cafes and a pub. Parking areas are good.

CAERBWDI BAY (30)

Caerbwdi Bay is a small sheltered beach of rock and pebble with sand visible at low tide. Close to St. Davids, it is reached along a half mile footpath leading from the A487 Solva to St. Davids road where there is limited parking. Although popular with walkers, the beach has no facilities.

CAERFAI BAY (31)

Caerfai Bay is the nearest beach to St. Davids and is popular with bathers, although at high tide the beach is covered leaving only rocks and boulders. A feature of the bay is the unusual purple sandstone along the cliffs, which was used to build St. Davids Cathedral. Parking is available above the beach, but there are no facilities.

WHITESANDS (32)

Whitesands, or to give is its Welsh name Traeth Mawr, is consistently rated one of Wales' very best seaside resorts. A large sandy beach in a magnificent setting,

Caerfai Bay

Newgale

Whitesands

Whitesands is well known for its views, glorious sunsets and crystal clear water. It is understandably popular with safe swimming and surfing areas designated by the lifeguards who patrol here during the summer months. If you can drag yourself away from the beach, there are some stunning walks with memorable views over the St. Davids Peninsula and Ramsey Island. Facilities at the beach are good and include a large car park. As an added bonus St. Davids, Britain's smallest city is close by with its many attractions and ancient cathedral.

PORTHMELGAN (33)

Porthmelgan is a sandy and secluded beach close to Whitesands. Access is along the coastal path from St. Davids or the car park at Whitesands.

ABEREIDDY BAY (34)

A few miles along the coast towards Fishguard will bring you to Abereiddy Bay which is vastly different to other beaches in the county in that it is covered in black sand. This is the result of waves constantly pounding the slate cliffs on either side. Tiny fossil graptolites are found in pieces of shale, which have geological importance and should not be removed. Nearby is the Blue Lagoon, a flooded slate quarry, which serves as a reminder that the area was quarried until 1904 when the slate was shipped all around Britain. A large car park overlooks the beach but bathers should take care when going into the waters because of undercurrents.

TRAETH LLYFN (35)

Half a mile away from Abereiddy is Traeth Llyfn, a beautiful sandy beach whose only access is down steep steps. The beach is enclosed by cliffs and can be dangerous for swimming, especially in rough seas because of strong undertows. There is also the possibility of getting cut off by the incoming tide.

TREFIN (36)

Trefin is not suitable for bathing because of rocks and an unstable cliff, but there are excellent walks and views along the coast in both directions. Above the beach where parking is very limited, there are the remains of an old mill.

Abereiddy

Trefin

Whitesands

Blue Lagoon

Abereiddy Bay

Trefin

Newport Sands

ABERCASTLE (37)

Abercastle is an attractive sheltered harbour much favoured by fishermen, boat enthusiasts and walkers. Picturesque cottages overlook the shingle beach, which has a small car park. Above the beach to the right lies Carreg Samson, a 4,500 year old burial chamber.

ABERMAWR (38)

Abermawr is a large sheltered beach covered in pebbles, which is rarely visited by lots of people. Access is along a short path from the road where parking is limited and although there are no other amenities, the beach is well worth visiting. Like other Pembrokeshire beaches the low tide reveals the remains of a drowned forest.

PWLLGWAELOD (39)

Pwllgwaelod near Dinas Head is a small attractive sandy beach with views of Fishguard Bay and its harbour. It offers good cliff walking, a nature trail and a linked path to the beach at Cwm-Yr-Eglwys.

CWM-YR-EGLWYS (40)

Overlooking the picturesque shingle and pebble beach are the remains of the 12th Century church of St. Brynach, which was destroyed during a fierce storm in 1859. The storm also wrecked over 100 ships. Access is along a narrow country lane off the main road between Fishguard and Cardigan, but is very much worth a visit. There is limited parking in a private car park.

NEWPORT PARROG (41)

The historic town of Newport stands near the mouth of the River Nevern where there are two beaches, one on either side of the estuary. The Parrog is on the southern side and although this is the more sheltered beach, unpredictable currents may make bathing dangerous. However the area is rich in prehistoric sites, including the Pentre Ifan burial chamber.

NEWPORT SANDS (42)

By far the more popular of Newport's two beaches, this vast expanse of sand on the northern side of the Nevern Estuary is backed by dunes and a golf course. A favourite spot for beach games and all manner of watersports, visitors should be careful of the dangerous currents around the mouth of the river. There's a car park above the beach and limited sand parking.

Pwllgwaelod

Newport

Newport Parrog

Newport

Beach safety advice from the RNLI

WHEREVER POSSIBLE, SWIM AT A LIFEGUARDED BEACH

READ AND OBEY THE SAFETY SIGNS USUALLY FOUND AT THE ENTRANCE TO THE BEACH

WHEN ON A LIFEGUARDED BEACH, FIND THE RED AND YELLOW FLAGS AND ALWAYS SWIM OR BODYBOARD BETWEEN THEM - THIS AREA IS PATROLLED BY LIFEGUARDS

NEVER SWIM ALONE

IF YOU GET INTO TROUBLE STICK YOUR HAND IN THE AIR AND SHOUT FOR HELP

IF YOU SEE SOMEONE IN DIFFICULTY, NEVER ATTEMPT A RESCUE. TELL A LIFEGUARD, OR IF YOU CAN'T SEE A LIFEGUARD, CALL 999 OR 112 AND ASK FOR THE COASTGUARD

FOR ALL IMPORTANT BEACH AND SAFETY INFORMATION VISIT: www.rnli.org.uk

CEIBWR BAY (43)

Ceibwr Bay is an ideal base for coastal walks as the area boasts the highest cliffs in Pembrokeshire. The spectacular coastal scenery includes the Witches Cauldron (a cave, blowhole and natural arch) together with incredible folding of the cliff rock strata. Another attraction is the sight of Atlantic grey seals swimming offshore or basking on the rocks. Access to Ceibwr Bay is along a narrow road from the village of Moylegrove with limited parking above the bay.

POPPIT SANDS (44)

Situated at the mouth of the Teifi Estuary, Poppit Sands is a large expanse of sand which marks the northern border of Pembrokeshire and the northern end of the Pembrokeshire Coastal Path. The proximity of the beach to the town of Cardigan has made it very popular with visitors. Bathers should be aware of dangerous currents and heed the warning signs and lifeguard flags. The beach is backed by sand dunes and mudflats, both of which are sensitive, fragile environments important to wildlife, so should be avoided. Facilities close to the beach are good and include a large car park.

Ceibwr Bay
Poppit Sands

THE SOUTH COAST

There are four main holiday centres in South Pembrokeshire: Tenby, Saundersfoot, Pembroke and Narberth. Tenby and its near neighbour Saundersfoot are among Britain's favourite seaside resorts, while the ancient town of Pembroke, which celebrated 900 years of history in 1993, boasts one of Britain's best preserved medieval castles. Narberth too is an historic town with a Norman castle. All four centres are close to the countless visitor attractions and places of interest, and each provides an ideal base for exploring the glorious South Pembrokeshire coastline and countryside.

TENBY

DISTANCES: Fishguard 36m; Haverfordwest 19m; Milford Haven; 19m; Narberth 10m; Pembroke 10m; St. Davids 35m; Saundersfoot 3m; Carmarthen 27m; London 247m

Little has changed in Tenby since wealthy Victorians provided the finance to develop the town into one of Britain's most attractive holiday resorts. The Victorians came here for the good of their health, but it was the birth of the coming railway in 1866 which saw a ground swell of visitors. Were those early visitors to return today, they would no doubt be surprised to discover that Tenby is almost as they had left it and has seemingly escaped what many would regard as the "plague" of modern development. Much of the 13th century wall which surrounds Tenby is still intact and the narrow streets, freshly recobbled to imitate a bygone age are still packed tight with shops and places to eat. Although the bathing machines have long gone, the beaches have still retained their appeal. Both the North Beach and South Beach are a mecca for holidaymakers. The picturesque harbour too is unchanged except for the boats. In Victorian time Tenby's link with the sea was dominated by the boats of a once thriving fishing industry as opposed to the leisure craft.

Tenby

Tenby

TENBY HARBOUR

Small, picturesque and brightly coloured by the neat painted cottages and spectrum of summer sail, Tenby harbour has a magnetic attraction. To sit on the harbour wall watching fishermen cast their lines and the boats sailing to and from Caldey Island is a pleasurable way of whiling away the time. Alternatively you can explore the lifeboat station passing Laston House on the way, where in the 19th century, Sir William Paxton played his part in helping to put Tenby on the map as a fashionable resort.

TUDOR MERCHANT'S HOUSE

Tenby's 15th century Tudor Merchant's House is the oldest furnished residence in the town. Standing on Quay Hill, between the harbour and Tudor square, its authentic furniture and fittings recreate the atmosphere of the period and illustrate the manner in which a successful Tudor merchant and his family would have lived. Three of the interior walls bear the remains of early Frescoes. Owned and managed by the National Trust, the house is open between March and October.

for further information call 01834 842279 or 01558 822800

TENBY LIFEBOAT STATION

Tenby is fortunate to have two lifeboats, the Hayden Miller and the smaller inshore rescue boat, the Georgina Stanley Taylor. The old lifeboat station, which is still standing, was established in 1852. The new lifeboat station is open to the public during the season for a fascinating insight into the workings of a modern lifeboat station. The new lifeboat, the Hayden Miller has been in operation since March 2006.

for further information go to www.tenby rnli.co.uk

TENBY MUSEUM AND GALLERY

Founded in 1878, Tenby Museum and Art Gallery is one of Tenby's main indoor attractions with the reputation of being one of the best local museums in the country. Situated on a spectacular site in part of the medieval castle, overlooking Castle Beach and Caldey Island. The galleries show the geology and archaeology of Pembrokeshire,its bygones and the changing aspects of Tenby's developments up to the present day. The art gallery concentrates on artists with close local associations and works by others which portray Tenby and its locality. Augustus John was born in Tenby and his sister Gwen, now highly regarded, was brought up here, there is also a permanent exhibition of their works. Other artists represented in the permanent collection include John Piper, David Jones, John Knapp-Fisher and Tenby born artist Nina Hamnett.

Please see the website for further details: www.tenbymuseum.org.uk

Tenby Museum and Art Gallery is open throughout the year. Partial access for disabled visitors. Research facilities. Admission charges and concessions apply, whilst refreshments are available.

Tenby Museum

Caldey Monastery

CALDEY ISLAND

A visit to Caldey Island is like stepping onto a different world. The monastery and ancient churches combine with the sea air and quiet, beautiful surroundings to create Caldey's unique atmosphere of timelessness and peace. Caldey is more than just an island with a monastery. You can enjoy a snack at the Tea Gardens, try the unique perfumes made on the island, visit the Chocolate Factory, choose an unusual gift or send a postcard franked with the island's special stamp. You can watch a video about the life of the monks and explore the Old Priory and the island's simple and inspiring churches. A walk up to the Lighthouse offers spectacular views of the Pembrokeshire coast and beyond. You can also follow the way-marked cliff and woodland paths, or simply relax on the sandy beach at Priory Bay. Caldey is a 20 minute boat trip from Tenby. Boats run every 20-30 minutes between 10am and 5pm from Easter to the end of October. Sailings are Monday to Saturday from May to September and Monday to Friday in April and October with selected Saturdays. A full range of products can be found at the Caldey Island shop, Quay Hill, Tenby.

Visit www.caldey-island.co.uk

TENBY PARKING

Around 50% of on street parking in Tenby is now reserved for residents (permits are £35 annually and need applying for), so our advice for parking in Tenby would be to head towards one of the car parks (none are free). There are 7 council run car parks and weekly and daily rates are available. There are designated motor cycle spaces at the Multi Storey in Tenby and disabled parking is available in all car parks but charges may apply so check on arrival.

There are also privately run car parks such as the Rectory car park above the South Beach. Many are seasonal but the Multi storey car park on Upper Park Road is open all year. Motor homes are permitted in the council car parks but cannot be slept in overnight (note height restrictions apply at both the Multi storey and the Salterns so motor homes would struggle with access at these two).

PENALLY

Nestling just west of Tenby is the pretty hillside village of Penally, which overlooks Tenby's golf course and South Beach. Penally is a well kept village complete with shop and pubs together with a good choice of accommodation including a first class hotel, the Penally Abbey, camping and caravan sites. A feature of the village is the 13th century church of St. Nicholas, which houses a memorial to the victims of the Tenby lifeboat who drowned when it capsized in 1834. Penally's proximity to Tenby, Lydstep, Manorbier, Freshwater East and Pembroke makes it an ideal holiday spot.

RITEC VALLEY QUAD BIKES, PENALLY

Ritec Valley Quad Bikes offers the ultimate in Quad bike entertainment whatever the weather, all year round.

Trail Riding is our serious activity (Minimum age 16) and needs to be booked in advance. We use 250cc semi-automatic sports quads (You need to be able to use gears).

We have over 12km of groomed routes to test every ability.

Arrive and Drive is for all ages

Arrive and Drive is for all ages and is carried out on Automatic quads (Minimum age 6). Arrive and Drive is for everyone under 16, families wishing to ride together or for seasoned quad bike addicts looking for a quick fix. No need to book, just Arrive and Drive.

We are open ALL YEAR but have a limited opening profile during the winter months.

For full info, please phone 01834 843390, or check out our website at: www.ritec-valley.co.uk Or email us on: thequadfather@btconnect.com

ST FLORENCE

Once a medieval harbour standing on an inlet to the sea, St. Florence is a picturesque village of great charm and pretty cottages and boasts a past winner of the national "Wales in Bloom" competition. Here you will discover one of the area's last surviving curious round chimneys, which are often described as Flemish in style. Also of interest is the 13th century parish church, featuring a Norman tower.

St. Florence

SAUNDERSFOOT

This bustling village is about three miles from Tenby, lying at the foot of a picturesque wooded valley. With its attractive harbour and extensive sandy beaches, it has established itself as a popular centre for sailing, fishing, watersports and traditional seaside holidays. Originally a small fishing village and home to two shipyards by the 1800's, Saundersfoot was suddenly caught up in the excitement of the black gold rush when high quality anthracite was discovered locally. Such was the demand for this coal that in 1829 the harbour was built, connected by rail to six mines. The railway ran along what is now The Strand and the coal was exported worldwide. It was not until the Second World War that coal shipments ceased, but by this time another flourishing industry was putting the village on the map - tourism. The rest they say is history.

Saundersfoot

THE NEW INN

OPEN ALL DAY MARCH - END OCTOBER
OPEN WEEKENDS IN WINTER

**REAL ALES * BAR FOOD * SUNDAY LUNCHES * 2 DINING ROOMS
FULL CHILDREN'S MENU * FRESH LOCAL FISH & BEEF
DISABLED ACCESS & TOILETS * DOGS ALLOWED IN BAR AREA
3 LOG BURNERS * TEAS & COFFEES * FANTASTIC VIEWS**

This family run charming 16th Century Inn is situated at the far end of Amroth which is at the start/end of the Pembrokeshire Coastal Path walk.

Real Ales are just one of our specialities offering 6 different types.

Our bar and restaurant menus offers only the finest in fresh local produce. Our homemade specials use only the best ingredients, including fresh local fish and Welsh beef from Pembrokeshire and Carmarthenshire

Outside there is a large beer garden beyond which lies ample car parking for patrons

A garden roof terrace which has the most amazing views of, Saundersfoot, Tenby and Caldey, which seats up too 20 people. Ideal for private parties

THE NEW INN
Amroth, Narberth, SA67 8NW

AMROTH AND PENDINE

The small coastal village of Amroth is just seven miles from Tenby and four miles from Saundersfoot. It is a wild and beautifully unspoiled location. In summer the wonderful expanse of gently shelving sand, exposed at low tide, makes it a favourite beach for families and anglers alike. The village, spread along the narrow seafront, has plenty of good facilities, including restaurants, pubs, gift shops, caravan parks and holiday homes. Attractions close by include Colby Woodland Garden, which is owned by the National Trust, and Pendine Sands, a resort made famous in the 1920's by speed king Sir Malcolm Campbell. In April 1926, Parry Thomas set a new World Land Speed record of 171.02mph driving his car "Babs". The following year he died at the wheel of "Babs" while attempting to regain the record. The car was buried in the sand by local villagers with the consent of his family and was recovered for restoration in March 1969.

Amroth

WISEMAN'S BRIDGE

A tiny hamlet, best known for its inn and rocky beaches, nestles on the coast between Saundersfoot and Amroth and at low tide it is possible to walk across the sands to either. You can also walk to Saundersfoot through the tunnels that once formed part of the all important railway link between local mines and Saundersfoot harbour.

KILGETTY

Before the bypass was built, the main road into South Pembrokeshire from the east went through Kilgetty village. However, the place remains an important centre for visitors, with its, railway station, and shops, it's also close to several major attractions. The neighbouring village of Begelly is well known for Folly Farm and is a short distance west of Kilgetty as are the villages of Broadmoor and East Williamston, where there are first class caravan parks and a pub.

STEPASIDE

It is hard to believe now but in the 19th century this quiet little hamlet was a hive of industrial activity after the Pembrokeshire Iron and Coal Company built the Kilgetty Ironworks here in 1848. Iron ore, in plentiful supply from seams along the cliffs between Amroth and Saundersfoot, was smelted in the blast furnace using locally produced limestone and coal and the iron transported to Saundersfoot harbour by railway.

COLBY WOODLAND GARDEN

Described by the National Trust as one of their most beautiful properties in Pembrokeshire, the garden is part of the Colby Estate, which was established by John Colby, the 19th century mining entrepreneur. The garden is a spectacular blaze of colour from early spring to the end of June. On site is a National Trust shop where refreshments are available, along with a gallery, plant sales, toilets and a car park.

for more information
01834 811885

Wiseman's Bridge

Wiseman's Bridge

Colby

Colby

Pembroke Dock

LONDON ROAD

TELEPHONE: 01646 687962

5am until 11pm SEVEN DAYS A WEEK

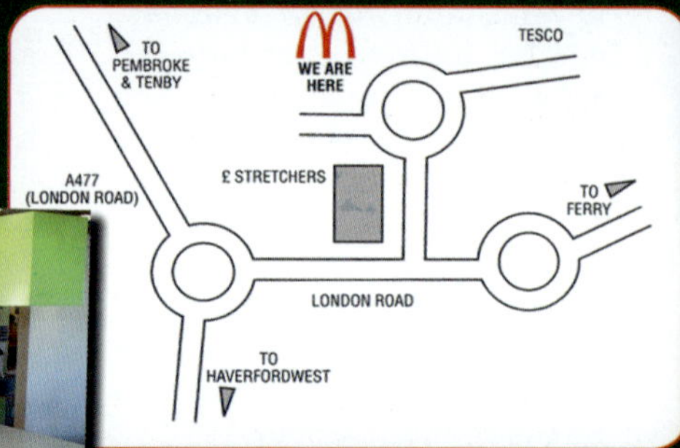

Haverfordwest

Drive Thru Open 24/7

CARADOCS WELL ROAD, MERLINS BRIDGE

TELEPHONE: 01437 769513

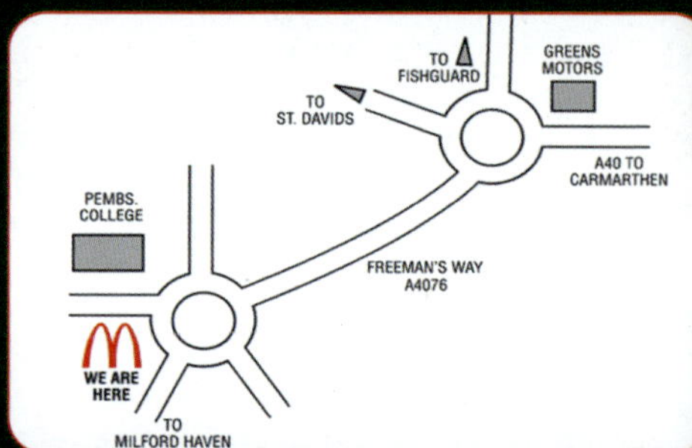

MANORBIER CASTLE

The stunning surroundings of Manorbier Castle offer a glimpse into a bygone age. Relax in our gardens and enjoy delicious light bites from our café. We are set on the coast path, just above the beautiful beach and within the National park.

Open from 10am to 5pm Every day during the season. Please check our website for any closures due to special events/weddings.

Dogs on leads welcome, parking at beach car park.

Admission: Adults £5.50, Children £3, Seniors £4. Family Ticket £15 (2 adults & 2 children)

www.manorbiercastle.co.uk
manorbiercastleoffice@gmail.com
Tel: 01834 870081

MANORBIER

Manorbier is a small seaside village midway between Tenby and Pembroke, and is best known for two striking features, the beach and a well preserved medieval castle. The castle, which enjoys a spectacular location overlooking the bay, was the birthplace of Gerald of Wales, a much respected medieval writer and a man of many talents whose two major works are still in print today. But Gerald wasn't the only one to find inspiration in Manorbier, George Bernard Shaw spent several months there, and prior to her marriage in 1912 Virginia Woolf was a regular summer visitor.

THE BIER HOUSE

The Bier House in the centre of the village was built in 1900 to house the parish bier, a funeral hand cart that was used to carry the dead to the burial ground. Now the building has been restored and provides an information point relating to the history of the parish.

LAMPHEY BISHOP'S PALACE

1 APRIL - 31 OCTOBER 2014
DAILY 10.00AM - 5.00PM
LAST ADMISSION 30 MINUTES BEFORE CLOSING

ADMISSION COSTS:
ADULT - £3.50 FAMILY - £10.50*
SENIOR CITIZENS, STUDENTS AND CHILDREN UNDER 16 - £2.65
DISABLED AND COMPANION - AM DDIM/FREE

UNDER 16S MUST BE ACCOMPANIED BY AN ADULT
DOGS ON LEADS WELCOME - NO SMOKING

LAMPHEY SA71 5NT - 01646 672224

LAMPHEY

Lamphey Palace

The village of Lamphey is the site of what is left of the Bishop's Palace, built in the 13th century by the Bishops of St. Davids and now in the care of Cadw who are responsible for Welsh Historic Monuments. The centuries old ruins are an evocative reminder of the great power enjoyed by the medieval Bishops of St. Davids. The comfortable palace buildings were set among well stocked fishponds, plump orchards and an extensive vegetable garden. In its heyday Lamphey boasted an impressive 144 acre park, a deer herd, windmill, two watermills and a dovecote. The palace's finest architectural features include the great hall built by Bishop Henry de Gower in the 14th century and the 16th century chapel.

for opening times and admission prices ring the Pembroke Library & Information Centre on 01437 776499 or CADW (Welsh Historic Monuments) on 01443 336000

PEMBROKE

DISTANCES: Fishguard 26m, Haverfordwest 10m, Milford Haven 5m, Narberth 15m St. Davids 26m, Tenby 12m, Carmarthen 32m, London 252m.

Pembroke is a small but charming walled town with a genteel atmosphere, a 900 year old history and much to recommend it to visitors. Like many other Welsh towns, Pembroke grew up around its medieval castle. This magnificent structure, the birthplace of Henry VII enjoys a spectacular location offering breathtaking views from the top of its famous keep. The castle is in a very good state of repair having undergone an extensive restoration programme that started as far back as 1928. Throughout the year the castle is the venue for many important events, several of which are traditions rooted firmly in the towns medieval past. The castle also plays host to such attractions including Shakespearean productions, medieval banquets, military tattoos and displays by the Sealed Knot Society.The Norman Conquest saw Pembroke develop into the main base from which the invaders increased their stranglehold on West Wales. The town became a major market centre with regular fairs. Now every October this tradition is still remembered when the town celebrates the Pembroke Fair which attracts visitors from far and wide.

One of the town's attractions is Mill Pond, formed by one of two tidal creeks. It's a popular beauty spot with visitors and locals alike because of the wildlife it attracts. Swans, herons, cormorants and if you are lucky enough even otters can be seen along this peaceful stretch of water. As visitors can explore Pembroke, they will see evidence of the town's ancient and extensive walls, which are a throw-back to the 13th century, when the townsfolk demanded that stone walls be built to protect their cottages from raiders. Under Norman rule, it established itself as an important trading port and hit a peak between the 17th and 19th centuries. In 1977, Pembroke was designated an outstanding Conservation Area.

Pembroke Castle

Pembroke Festival

EDU TOYS @ PEMBROKE POST OFFICE

Edu Toys @ Pembroke Post Office is renowned for its unique range of educational and wooden toys together with fabulous children's clothing. Our toys have proven to be a winner with both children and adults alike! We are constantly on the look out for new products and have recently introduced a fabulous range of wooden train sets. Childrenswear is also popular for those who like something a little different. Fabulous dresses for girls up to age 4 for that special occasion (or simply to look pretty!) are a must to see. We are the only stockist of Sarah Louise in Pembrokeshire. So it's something different you are looking for, pop in and see us

or visit us on

Facebook – edutoyspembroke

tel: 01646 682737

PEMBROKE VISITOR CENTRE

Built in 1993 to coincide with the town's 900th birthday celebrations, this is an integral part of Pembroke's superb new Tourist Information Centre. Displays and exhibits tell the story of Pembroke and there is a choice of books, maps and souvenirs on sale.

tel: 01437 776499

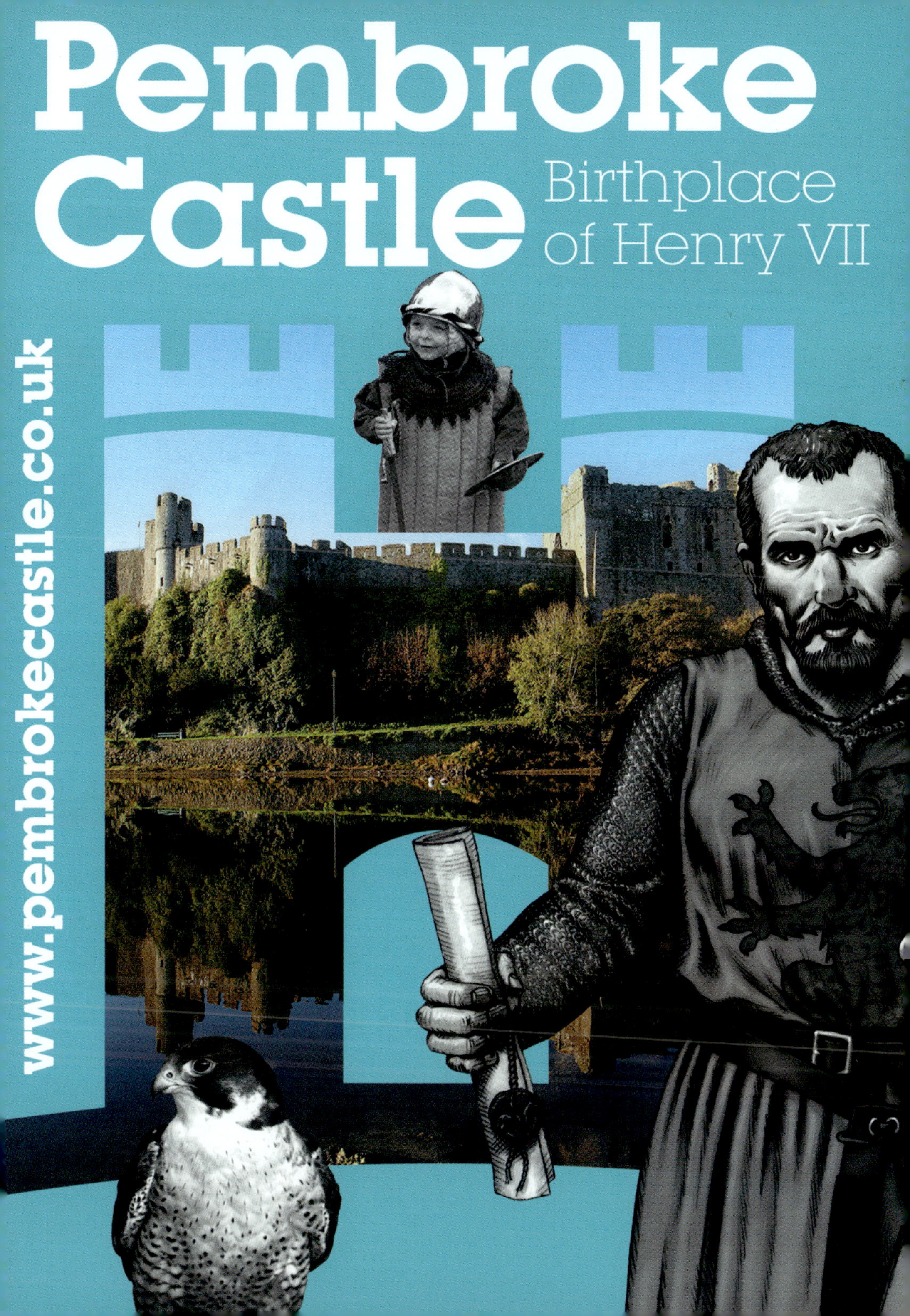
Pembroke Castle
Birthplace of Henry VII
www.pembrokecastle.co.uk

PEMBROKE DOCK

In the early 19th century it was nothing more than a small coastal village known as Paterchurch. But when in 1814 the lease expired on the Royal Naval Dockyard in Milford Haven, the Admiralty decided to move its shipbuilding operation across the water and further from the mouth of the estuary and Paterchurch was designated the ideal site. Hence began an amazing transformation, which saw naval architects lay out the distinctive grid pattern of wide streets so characteristic of today's Pembroke Dock. In 1930 a major part of the dockyard site was transferred from the Admiralty to the Air Ministry, and in the following year the Royal Air Force established a seaplane base, operated by Southampton flying boats of 210 Squadron.

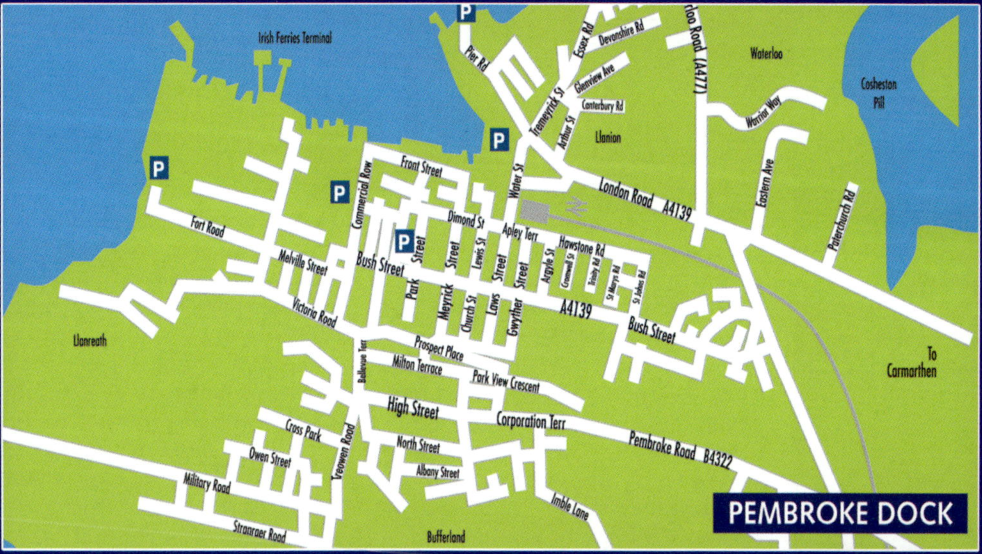

1938 saw the arrival of the first Sunderland flying boat, the aircraft with which Pembroke Dock is most associated. During the Second World War the Sunderlands gave sterling service and eventually stayed on here until 1957. In March 1993, during one of the lowest tides of the century, three men discovered the remains of a rear gun turret and fairing, part of a Sunderland flying boat of 201 Squadron that crashed in the Haven Waterway during a training exercise in March 1954. Today Pembroke Dock is better known as a ferry port with excellent boating and watersport facilities.

THE GUN TOWER MUSEUM

The Gun Tower formed part of the fortifications of the Milford Haven waterway. The tower's specific role was to help defend and protect the Royal Naval Dockyard, though in the event the only threat came from the air raids in the Second World War, long after the dockyard had closed.Built in 1851 to repel "unwelcome guests", the imposing dressed stone tower now welcomes visitors with open arms. Visitors are offered an intriguing experience of the life lived by Queen Victoria's soldiers and marines, who waited, in these cramped quarters, for the French invasion that never came. Three floors of colourful models, pictures and full scale displays include life sized soldiers and many authentic relics. A splendid panoramic model shows us the town's Royal Dockyard. Here 250 warships were built, along with five elegant Royal yachts. During World War Two, Pembroke Dock was the world's largest operational flying boat base. Important features include an original working roof cannon and the basement magazine, where 20,000 lbs of gunpowder were stored, plus an educational video.

for all information
call: 01646 622246

Green Bridge of Wales

THE CASTLEMARTIN PENINSULA

The Castlemartin Peninsula, which is also known as the Angle Peninsula, typifies the unique appeal of South Pembrokeshire in that it has many special features of interest to many different groups. Birdwatchers flock here for the many colonies of species that nest along the cliffs and rock formations. There are outstanding examples of fissures, sea caves, blowholes, natural arches and stacks. Anthropologists have been excited by the discovery of bones and implements in caves which 20, 000 years ago gave shelter to the region's earliest known human inhabitants. Historians are enchanted by such mysteries as tiny St. Govan's Chapel and by the remains of Iron Age Forts and other ancient sites. For visitors who are here to simply enjoy a holiday, there are attractions such as the Bosherston Lily Ponds and the superb beaches of Barafundle, Broad Haven, Freshwater West and West Angle Bay to savour. The peninsula is also well known for its 6000 acre Ministry of Defence tank range. This means that a large section of the coastline is inaccessible, one of the very few places in Pembrokeshire that the coast path is diverted inland.

FRESHWATER EAST

From the small coastal village of Freshwater East, visitors are ideally placed to explore the stunning coastline. Freshwater East is a popular resort in its own right. The Trewent Park holiday complex provides self-catering accommodation close to the beach and there is a touring caravan park.

STACKPOLE

Stackpole has its name in Norse origins, and the village as it stands today is in a different place from its original medieval site, The centre of the old village is about half a mile to the southwest, marked by the remains of a preaching cross.

STACKPOLE QUAY

The National Trust owns and manages Stackpole Quay, which it acquired in 1976 as part of the 2000 acres of Stackpole Estate. This acquisition also included the stretch of coastline between here and Broad Haven, under the Enterprise Neptune initiative, a scheme launched in 1965 to save and protect Britain's precious and threatened coastline. Stackpole Quay was originally a private quay built for the estate, so that coal could be imported and limestone shipped out from the quarry. It is claimed that this is Britain's smallest harbour, however pleasure boats are now the only craft that use the stone jetty.

Bosherston

STACKPOLE QUARRY

As part of its management of the Stackpole Estate, the National Trust has utilised the natural geological features of the old quarry near Stackpole Quay to create an area in which visitors, including those with special needs, can enjoy countryside recreation. Around the top of the quarry is a circular path giving spectacular vistas of the surrounding landscape and coastline. Down below, on the quarry floor, are sheltered picnic and barbecue areas and an archery bay. In addition, the cleared rock faces a present a challenge to experienced climbers and abseilers. Everyone can use the quarry's facilities, but groups or event organisers should first contact the warden. Close to the quarry is the main car park for Stackpole Quay, along with the National Trust holiday cottages, carefully converted from old buildings.

for more information about holiday letting call 0870 458411 or visit www.nationaltrust.org.uk for details of the quarry facilities call 01646 661359

BOSHERSTON

For such a small village, Bosherston certainly enjoys its fair share of fame due to its proximity to several major tourist attractions in South Pembrokeshire. These include the delightful Bosherston Lily Ponds, part of the Stackpole Lakes, and Broad Haven beach. On days when the M.O.D tank range is not in use and the access roads are open, Bosherston is also the gateway to the remarkable St. Govan's Chapel and some of the best limestone cliff scenery in Europe, with coastal features such as St. Govan's Head, Huntsman's Leap, Stack Rocks and the Green Bridge of Wales.

Lily Ponds

The village is also home to the 14th century St.Michael's Church which has an unusual cross of the same period standing in the churchyard. Much older still is a huge boulder, originating from Scotland, which was deposited at Bosherston by a moving glacier during the last Ice Age. Bosherston also has ample parking, with alternative parking above Broad Haven, and a pub, tearooms and toilets. When the tank range access road is open there is also plenty of free parking at St. Govan's.

to find out range road access times ask at any Tourist Information Centres or ring Merrion Camp on 01646 662287 or Bosherston Tearooms on 01646 661216.

BOSHERSTON LILY PONDS AND BROAD HAVEN

When the Campbells of Stackpole created the lakes and lily ponds to enhance their estate in the late 18th and early 19th centuries, they were unwittingly setting the scene for an attraction that brings thousands of annual visitors to the small village of Bosherston. Covering more than 80 acres, the lakes and lily ponds are the largest area of fresh water in the Pembrokeshire Coast National Park and are part of the Stackpole National Nature Reserve. They are usually at their very best around June, when the lilies are in full bloom, but even in winter they provide easy and fascinating walks. They also offer good coarse fishing and are well stocked with roach, pike, tench and eels. Fishing permits are available from the tearooms in the village. There are in fact three lakes, artificially created by the deliberate flooding of narrow limestone valleys. The lily ponds occupy only the western lake, which is fed by underwater springs. Grey herons are regular visitors, and the total lakes area attracts a great variety of birds and wildlife, including coots, moorhens, mallard, teal, swans, cormorants, kingfishers, buzzards and many smaller winged visitors such as blue damseflies and emperor dragonflies. Over 20 species of duck alone have been recorded here.

Lilies in bloom

Broad Haven

Vi's Tearooms

Broad Haven

St Govans Head

ST. GOVAN'S CHAPEL

Remarkable St. Govan's Chapel is one of the wonders of Pembrokeshire. A tiny building hidden in a fissure in the cliff near St. Govan's car park, the restored chapel nestles at the bottom of a flight of narrow steps. It is said that if you count the steps on the way down and then count them on the way back up, the numbers won't tally. Though it occupies the site of a 5th century hermit's cell, the age of the chapel itself is not known for sure; expert estimates put it at no older than 11th century. St. Govan is reputedly buried beneath the altar. It is also said that Sir Gawaine, one of King Arthur's Knights, lived here in isolation. Yet another legend tells of the holy well's miraculous healing powers. St. Govan's Chapel is close to St. Govan's Head, the most southerly point in Pembrokeshire and is well worth seeing for its dramatic cliff scenery.

HUNTSMAN'S LEAP

According to legend, a horseman fleeing from pursuers miraculously leaped across this gaping chasm in the cliffs west of St. Govan's Chapel. On looking back he was so horrified by the prospect of what might have happened that the shock killed him anyway.

GREEN BRIDGE OF WALES

Standing just 150 yards or so from Stack Rocks car park, the Green Bridge of Wales is an excellent example of a natural limestone arch. It was formed by the joining of two caves, each created by erosion of the rock by constant bombardment by the sea, and eventually the roof of the arch will collapse and leave a pinnacle of rock, a stack standing in the sea. This is the same process that created Stack Rocks. The Green Bridge of Wales is easy to see and photograph in full profile with complete safety thanks to the wooden viewing platform constructed especially for the purpose by the National Park Authority.

Green Bridge

Stack Rocks

St Govans Head

St Govans Chapel

the WHERE TO EAT guide

Restaurant Key

PEMBROKESHIRE PRODUCE ACCREDITED

LICENSED

DISABLED FRIENDLY

FAMILY FRIENDLY

PARKING

(10) MAP REF FOUND ON PAGE 3

(1) MAP PG 3 — THE GILTAR HOTEL

9 ESPLANADE, TENBY, SA70 7DU, Tel: 01834 842507
www.giltar-hotel.co.uk

Come and relax in our beautiful restaurant overlooking the sea towards Caldey. We are open for lunches and dinner in the evening, as well as the traditional Sunday Lunch.

SEE ADVERT PAGE 20

(60) MAP PG 3 — CAFE MOR

Cafe Môr is the name given to our street food outlet at Freshwater West beach in South Pembrokeshire.In 2014 Cafe Môr won the BBC Food & Farming award for 'Best Street food/Take Away in the UK' and earlier, in 2011 it was awarded 'Best of the Best' at The British Street Food Awards. From 2015 onward we started doing something spectacular. We became the second of only two mobile food outlets in the UK (both from Pembrokeshire) to power their kitchens using solar & wind energy. Hello sustainable energy, goodbye noisy generator!

(1) MAP PG 3 — THE NORMANDIE

UPPER FROG ST, TENBY, SA70 7JD,
Tel: 01834 842227
www.normandietenby.co.uk

A vibrant, colourful bar and restaurant with rooms nestled between the Historic Town Walls and Upper Frog Street. Emphasis is on great food, wines and beers and excellent accommodation.

1 MAP PG 3 FIVE ARCHES TAVERN & RESTAURANT

ST GEORGE'S ST, TENBY, SA70 7JB, Tel: 01834 842513

A highly recommended venue with a warm welcome serving a variety of homemade dishes on the menu.

five arches tavern and restaurant

SEE ADVERT PAGE 18

1 MAP PG 3 BLUEBERRY'S

HIGH STREET, TENBY, SA70 7EU W: www.blueberrystenby.co.uk
E: eat@blueberrystenby.co.uk T: 01834 845785

Welcome to Blueberry's. We are an independent run Cafe/Restaurant, giving flexibility of choice to please our customers, where others may not.

2 MAP PG 3 PENALLY ABBEY

PENALLY, NR TENBY, SA70 7PY, Tel: 01834 843033
www.penally-abbey.com

Delicious, unpretentious food in beautiful surroundings.

THE LYDSTEP TAVERN

MAP PG 3 **3**

LYDSTEP, TENBY, SA70 7SG, Tel: 01834 871521

Good food and fine ale in a traditional country inn.

SEE ADVERT PAGE 34

THE BUSH INN

Canaston Bridge, Robeston Wathen,SA678EP
Tel 01834 860778, www.the bush-inn.co.uk

We have earned a glowing reputation for the quality of the food served here which is based as far as possible on fresh wholesome local produce.

SEE ADVERT PAGE 159

THE NEW INN

MAP PG 3 **55**

AMROTH, NARBERTH, PEMBS, SA67 8NW
Tel: 01834 812368, www.newinnamroth.co.uk

Family run charming 16th Century Inn, serving bar/restaurant food, specialising in fresh local produce. Tea's, coffees and full children's menu available

SEE ADVERT PAGE 28

WISEMAN'S BRIDGE INN

MAP PG 3 **19**

WISEMAN'S BRIDGE, SAUNDERSFOOT, SA69 9AU
Tel: 01834 813236, www.wisemansbridgeinn.co.uk

The setting for this traditional pub couldn't be better. Enjoy a meal or even just a quiet drink whilst taking in the superb sweeping views of Carmarthen Bay, either from our dining room or from our garden that extends right down to the beach. A range of real ales is on offer, together with a bar snack and evening meals menu.

54 MAP PG 3 — THE DIAL INN

RIDGEWAY ROAD, LAMPHEY, SA71 5NU WALES
01646 672 426, dialinn@btconnect.com

An elegant, interesting and deceptively large village pub has excellent bar food and wine list, plus an imaginative evening menu, freshly prepared and cooked.

7 MAP PG 3 — THE CLEDDAU BRIDGE HOTEL

ESSEX ROAD, PEMBROKE DOCK, SA72 6EG, Tel: 01646 685961
www.cleddauhotel.co.uk

Excellent a la carte restaurant serving high quality locally sourced fare, combining a superb menu with fantastic waterway views.

SEE ADVERT INSIDE REAR COVER

58 MAP PG 3 — WAVECREST CAFE

WEST ANGLE BAY SA71 5BE - 07791 888479
www.wavecrestangle.co.uk

Magnificent beachside location
Local crab & lobster * Fresh Baked Baguettes *Homemade cakes * Local Beers & Cider * Local Ice Cream
Blackboard Specials

SEE ADVERT PAGE 44

7 MAP PG 3 — MCDONALDS

LONDON ROAD, PEMBROKE DOCK, SA72 6BP
Tel: 01646 687962

Excellent quality food for the family in a hurry.
Recently refurbished restaurant and with drive thru facility.

SEE ADVERT PAGE 32

THE CAREW INN

MAP PG 3 40

THE CAREW INN, CAREW, TENBY, SA70 8SL
Tel: (01646) 651267 www.carewinn.co.uk

Open All Day throughout the year. Food is served every lunch time and every evening throughout the year

CAREW ·INN·

THE BRISTOL TRADER

MAP PG 3 9

QUAY ST, HAVERFORDWEST, SA61 1BE,
TEL 01437 76 21 22

Our full menu is served from 12-8.30 pm Monday to Thursday, and 7 pm on Friday and Saturday. On Sundays come and join us for our famous carvery, we have three sittings, between 12 & 3pm. Bookings are advised.

MCDONALDS

MAP PG 3 9

CARADOCS WELL ROAD,HAVERFORDWEST, SA61 1XJ
Tel: 01437 769513

Excellent quality food for the family in a hurry. Recently refurbished restaurant and with drive thru facility.

SEE ADVERT PAGE 32

McDonald's ™

11 MAP PG 3 THE REFECTORY AT ST DAVIDS CATHEDRAL

ST DAVIDS CATHEDRAL, THE CLOSE, ST DAVIDS, SA62 6PE
Tel: 01437 721760 www.stdavidscathedral.org.uk

We serve delicious food and drink in one of the most beautiful spaces in Wales. Our lunch menu changes daily and we always have freshly made sandwiches and cakes on offer, plus excellent tea and coffee.
We are also a licensed premises.

THE REFECTORY at ST DAVIDS

11 MAP PG 3 ORIEL Y PARC CAFE

THE VISITOR CENTRE, ST DAVIDS SA62 6NW
01437 721512 OR 720392 www.orielyparc.co.uk

Opening Hours: Nov-Feb Mon -Sat 10-4 Feb-Oct 7 days 9-5.30
Serving breakfast, lunch and cakes with access to gift shop & art gallery.
Evening events and buffets catered for also. Gluten free options available!

12 MAP PG 3 THE SLOOP INN

PORTHGAIN, SA62 5BN Tel: 01348 831449

The Sloop Inn, probably the best known pub in the county, is situated just 100 yards from the harbour of Porthgain. The menu is varied, catering for all tastes including vegetarians and children.
A full menu is available 12.00 - 2.30 & 6.00 - 9.30 every day including specials, Sunday Lunches, plus limited choice in the afternoon high season.

24 MAP PG 3 CWM DERI VINEYARD AND ESTATE

MARTLETWY, SA67 8AP, Tel: 01834 891274

Whether it is a simple cup of coffee and cake, a cream tea or a full meal, the restaurant and cafe at Cwm Deri can satisfy your needs. Using only the finest ingredients from Pembrokeshire wherever possible. Our chef Daniel can cater the food requirements of individuals or for parties of up to forty or more. Enjoy a tasting of our wines and liqueurs, either in our shop or on our patio and terrace, with a commanding view over the vineyard.

SEE ADVERT PAGE 174

Cwm Deri Vineyard and ESTATE

17 MAP PG 3

FIRE & ICE

66 ST JAMES STREET, NARBERTH, SA67 7DB

A selection of locally produced ice creams in 12 fantastic flavours. Dairy free Sorbets, Sugar free & Gluten free available.

Take Home Tubs available (0.75ltr & 1ltr) flavours change weekly.

FIRE & ICE

A Delicious Selection Of Locally Produced Ice Creams

23 MAP PG 3

LLYS-Y-FRAN RESERVOIR RESTAURANT & TEAROOMS

CLARBESTON ROAD,HAVERFORDWEST, SA63 4RR, Tel: 01437 532694

With beautiful views and a sun patio that's open during the summer months. A function room is available for wedding receptions, private parties, seminars etc. please ring for further details

SEE ADVERT PAGE 149

Llys-Y-Fran COUNTRY PARK & RESERVOIR

17 MAP PG 3

(NARBERTH) THE CREATIVE CAFE (HAVERFORDWEST)

MAP PG 3 9

SPRING GARDENS, NARBERTH
PEMBROKESHIRE SA67 7BT
Tel: 01834 861651

22 HIGH ST, HAVERFORDWEST
PEMBROKESHIRE SA61 2DA
TEL: 01437 766698

The Creative Café is a paint-your-own pottery studio with a difference - where YOU can be the artist... whether you're artistic or not! Come and create your very own ceramic masterpiece in either of our two studios.

NARBERTH ONLY

THE CREATIVE CAFÉ paint your own pottery Narberth & Haverfordwest

13 MAP PG 3

THE FARMERS ARMS

MATHRY, NR FISHGUARD, SA62 5HB
Tel: 01348 831284,
www.farmersarmsmathry.co.uk

Good food and fine ale in a traditional country inn.

43 MAP PG 3 PENRALLT GARDEN CENTRE

MOYLEGROVE, CARDIGAN, SA43 3BX
Tel: 01239 881295, www.penralltnursery.co.uk

Enjoy a freshly prepared meal at our Pavilion Cafe. Morning Coffee Lunches, Afternoon Teas. Our menu includes an excellent range of home made cakes and savoury dishes. The Pavilion scones with jam and welsh clotted cream is a must have, along with our range of teas and freshly ground coffee.

SEE ADVERT PAGE 134

15 MAP PG 3 THE ROYAL OAK NEWPORT CURRY HOUSE

WEST STREET, NEWPORT, SA42 0TA, Tel: 01239 820632

Established as the "Curry House" of Newport, we also specialise in fresh fish and grills, using local produce wherever possible. Vegetarians & special diets are catered for and traditional Sunday Lunch is served all year round.

SEE ADVERT PAGE 130

30 MAP PG 3 QUAYSIDE LAWRENNY TEAROOM

LAWRENNY QUAY, LAWRENNY, SA68 0PR
Tel: 01646 651574

Fantastic innovative menu with a variety of dishes made from fresh local produce, most notably local crab and shellfish, with unparalleled waterside views.

SEE ADVERT PAGE 172

8 MAP PG 3 CAFE TORCH (TORCH THEATRE)

TORCH THEATRE, ST. PETER'S ROAD, MILFORD HAVEN, SA73 2BU
www.torchteatre.co.uk, Tel: 01646 695267

Open daily for lunches, sandwiches, snacks and homemade cakes, it's also a great meeting place. In our modern, comfy surroundings you can enjoy a bit of peace and quiet, a great terrace to sit out on when the weather is fine and WiFi access makes it suitable for a quiet working lunch.

CAFÉ TORCH CAFFI
WiFi Hotspot

SEE ADVERT PAGE 83

ATTRACTIONS

Pembrokeshire is fortunate to have many top class attractions which will enhance any holiday whatever the weather. There are top family attractions such as Folly Farm, Oakwood Theme Park, The Dinosaur Park, Heatherton and Manor House Wildlife Park now owned by Anna Ryder Richardson. If the weather takes a turn for the worst then the Blue Lagoon development at Bluestone offers the best in wet fun under a dry roof. Contained within this section is a guide to all of the best attractions that Pembrokeshire has to offer to suit all tastes and ages.

www.annaswelshzoo.co.uk
MANOR HOUSE
TENBY'S FAVOURITE
WILDLIFE PARK
fourzooNique
animalwalkthroughs
For a life-changing experience
shadowkeeper
pre-book on: 01646 651201
ANNA'S
WELSH ZOO
AS SEEN ON
BBC
itv Wales
ANIMAL PLANET
S4/C
real fun real food
real experience
ST FLORENCE,TENBY, SA70 8RJ
01646 - 651201
gate@annaswelshzoo.co.uk
OPEN 363 DAYS A YEAR
GET CLOSER THAN EVER TO ENDANGERED SPECIES

WATERFALL ★ MINI-GOLF ★ SNAKE RIVER FALLS ★ MOON LANDING ★ BOBSLEIGH ★ CIRCUS LAND
SIGHTS OF LONDON ★ JOLLY ROGER ★ LOST BOYS ADVENTURE ★ NEVERLAND CHASE ★ CROCODILE COASTER
You Tube
JOURNEY TO NEVERLAND
Wales' BIGGEST Family Adventure!
NEW
NEVERLAND
BELIEVE IN DREAMS
TINK'S FLYING SCHOOL
FAMILY RIDE
TREE TOPS!
PHOTOS NOW AVAILABLE
Ride SKULL ROCK
THE ORIGINAL AFTER DARK
AUGUST WEDS & SATS Open 'til 10pm
FAMILY ★ FRIENDLY ★ FUN

It's the YEAR OF ADVENTURE in WALES
Start YOUR adventure at
Award-winning OUTDOOR LASER COMBAT
BATTLEFIELD
PEMBROKESHIRE
RESPAWN
AMMO RECHA

Award Winning Activity

ULTIMATE LASER COMBAT GAME

10 mins from Tenby and 15 mins from Carmarthen

Fun and outdoor adventure awaits you at Wales' premier laser combat site. Take part in exciting missions in our purpose-built, atmospheric, jungle-themed 'battlefield'. The most fun you'll ever have dressed in camo gear.

Battlefield Pembrokeshire Laser Combat has all the adrenalin-fuelled fun of Call of Duty but without the sofa; it has all the fun of paintball without the pain; and it makes for a great day out with the family. Our fully trained marshals are professional, friendly and on hand at all times.

We also offer awesome BIRTHDAY PARTIES for all ages.
Check out our website for the latest deals
www.battlefieldlivepembrokeshire.co.uk

Accredited by Visit Wales as a quality attraction, award-winning Battlefield Pembrokeshire Laser Combat is the first activity you will encounter as you enter Pembrokeshire (heading towards Tenby).

Fun and adventure awaits you in atmospheric, jungle-themed woodland. The most fun you will ever have dressed in camo gear. Take part in exciting missions run by experienced, fully trained and friendly marshals where you will have loads of fun, laughs and adrenalin rushes. This is a great day out and will provide lasting memories

Recent review from a visiting family:

This place was absolutely fantastic! We had a family group which included ages between 10-70 and even the teenagers loved it ~ everyone came home smiling & weeks later are still talking about it. The staff were exceptionally friendly & organised, clear & helpful. The layout for the missions covered a large, varied area & were well designed. The 'weapons' were accurate & reliable with options for 'sniper rifles' available in certain missions. The outfits were clean and fitted well. Some of our group waited at the reception area (whilst the battle took place) and were looked after by staff with refreshments. The facilities were portakabins near reception. Parking was easy. We would definitely recommend this place & look forward to going again.

It's the Year of Adventure in Wales so start your adventure with us and immerse yourself in the exciting experience that is Battlefield Pembrokeshire Laser Combat.

Sessions run at 11am, 1.30pm and 4pm. Minimum age is 7

WHY DO WE USE INFRA-RED?

- **More accurate than paintball**
- **Reaches longer distances than paintball**
- **More tactical than paint-ball**
- **Safer than paintball**
- **No cheating**
  Environmentally friendly
- **No long waits - you get respawned straight back into the action**
- **No extra charges for ammo**

You can BOOK by phone - 07777671301

by email - pembslivegaming@btinternet

or via the contact form on our website
www.battlefieldlivepembrokeshire.co.uk

Clerkenhill
Adventure Farm
and Frizbee Golf Course

Clerkenhill Adventure
Slebech, Haverfordwest
SA62 4PE
Tel: 01437 751227
www.clerkenhill.co.uk

LOTS OF INDOOR FUN

Follow the safe adventure trail through the spooky woodland

Have a chat with the animals around the park.

Watch the children laughing and playing in the numerous large play areas

18 basket Frizbee Golf course spread over 10 acres and surrounded by beautiful countryside with trees and streams

NEW FUN PARTY ROOM

CAFE & SHOP

Clerkenhill Adventure Farm's "Adventure Castle" incorporates many different slides, tunnel walks, rope and wobble bridges, dungeons and secret hideouts.

Scolton Manor

COUNTY MUSEUM, MANOR HOUSE, TEA ROOM, ECO-CENTRE AND SHOP

A traditional Victorian country house, Scolton Manor was home to successive generations of the Higgon family, until it was bought by Pembrokeshire County Council in 1972.

The Manor House has been sympathetically restored by the Museum Service in order to provide visitors with a taste of Victorian society and style, both above and below stairs.

New at Scolton this year will be a unique Beekeeping Centre run by Pembrokeshire Beekeepers' Association.

The site, which will initially play host to 10 hives, will enable the public to see a working apiary in action. The centre will also include a honey kitchen, where honey will be processed, bottled and sold to the public.

The planned proposals are a key part of the County Council's vision for the re-development of the old Victorian estate where work has already started on the restoration of the Walled Garden.

The 60 acres of park and woodland surrounding Scolton Manor have been used as a country park for since the 1970s. As the only site in Pembrokeshire to have achieved a Green Flag Award, the Museum Service is keen to manage the park in a way that continually encourages and conserves wildlife, as well as creating opportunities to enjoy and experience its variety.

Scolton is developing as an outdoors 'green gym' helping to support an active lifestyle. Why not come along and try out our two exciting activity trails – Dragon's Run, the mini-beast exercise trail, and the Power Plant tree trail. Discovery and fun for everyone

Located at the bottom of the park, near the car parks, the Visitor Centre and Park Warden's office. Toilets ar baby changing facilities are also to be found within th building.

The Tearooms can be found next to the manor house and are open seven days a week. Light lunches and snacks are served all day, and local Welsh produce is used where possible.

For children, there's a great recreational area towards the bottom of the park, including a wooden adventure play area, swings and slide – plus picnic tables for m and dad to have a sit in the sun!

Dogs on leads are welcome in the park.

OPENING TIMES
Every day except Christmas Day/Boxing Day:
April - October
9.00am - 6.00pm
November - March
9.00am - 4.30pm

MUSEUM:
Open every day
10.30am - 5.30pm
April - October

HOW TO FIND US:
5 miles north of Haverfordwest on the B4329 Cardigan Road

MUSEUM 01437 731328

PARK 01437 731457

ATTRACTION LISTINGS

BATTLEFIELD LIVE
Tel: 07777 671301

BLUE LAGOON
Tel: 01834 862410

CAREW KARTING
Tel: 07974540689

CASTELL HENLLYS
Tel: 01239 891319

CLERKENHILL ADVENTURE FARM
Tel: 01437 751227

CWM DERI VINEYARD
Tel: 01834 891274

THE DINOSAUR PARK
Tel: 01834 845272

FOLLY FARM
Tel: 01834 812731

HEATHERTON SPORTS PARK
Tel: 01646 652000

LLYS-Y-FRAN COUNTRY PARK
Tel: 01437 532694

MANOR HOUSE WILD ANIMAL PARK
Tel: 01646 651201

OAKWOOD THEME PARK
Tel: 01834 891373

PALACE CINEMA
Tel:01437 767675

RITEC VALLEY QUAD BIKES
Tel: 01834 843390

SCOLTON MANOR
Tel: 01437 731328

TORCH THEATRE
Tel: 01646 695267

WEST WALES KARTING
Tel: 01437 769555

THE WEST COAST

Pembrokeshire's Atlantic West Coast is a wild and dramatic landscape of spectacular cliff scenery, golden beaches and secluded coves. Offshore are the nearby islands of Skomer and Skokholm and much further out to sea, Grassholm, names which are a reminder of the days when ransacking Viking war lords and Norse settlers made their mark in the area. Not surprisingly, Haverfordwest has increasingly become a major holiday base for visitors to the Dale Peninsula, Marloes Peninsula, St. Bride's Bay and even the Preseli Hills. Indeed, it is ideally placed for exploring the whole of Pembrokeshire.

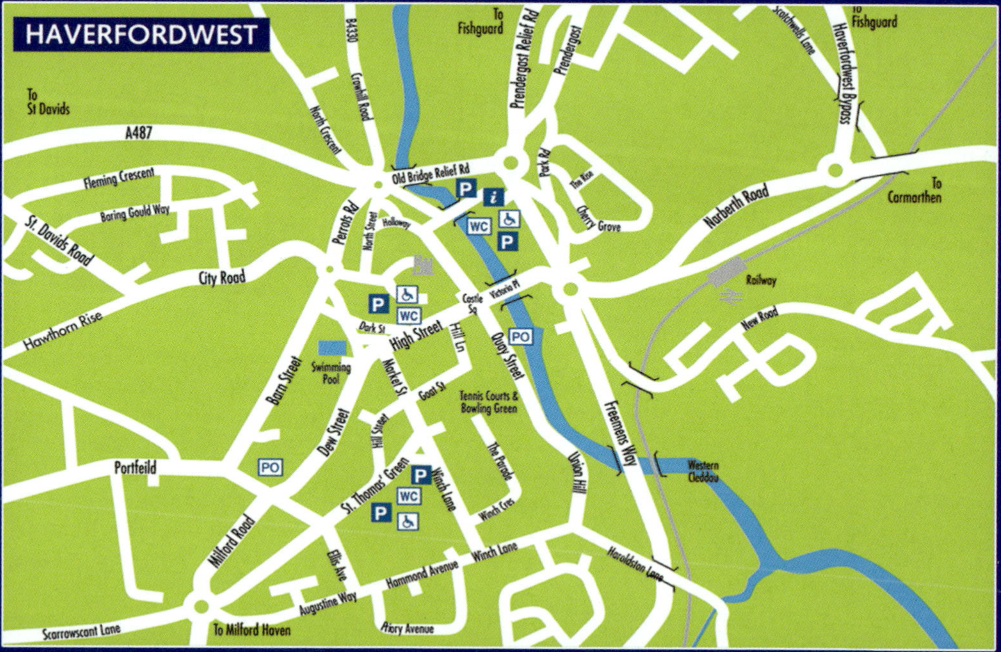

HAVERFORDWEST

DISTANCES: Fishguard 16m, Milford Haven 7m, Narberth 8m, Pembroke 11m, St. Davids 16m, Tenby 19m, Carmarthen 30m, and London 245m

Overlooking the town centre are the ruins of the medieval castle. The centre itself has a medieval street plan, but the first appearances suggest that the only buildings older than 18th century are the castle and three Norman churches of St. Mary's, St. Martin's and St. Thomas's. However, behind the new facades of many buildings are much older structures. The keep and substantial sections of wall are all that remain of the castle today. In the 18th and 19th centuries it was used as a gaol, until the new county gaol was built in 1820. It has also been a police station. St. Mary's Church is one of South Wales' finest. Built in the 13th century but substantially altered in the 15th century, it has many outstanding features, including curved oak roofs, a brass dating back to 1651 and an early English lancet window. St. Martin's with its high steeple, is the town's oldest church and has undergone much restoration. From Tudor times to the early part of this century Haverfordwest was a flourishing port. The decline of the port is a familiar story in 19th century

Riverside Quay, Haverfordwest

Wales. In 1853 the arrival of the first train in Haverfordwest was greeted with great celebration. travel had dawned and shipping could not compete. Today, the once hectic quay has become the Riverside Quay Shopping Centre. A modern and attractive development, it includes a large indoor market a reminder that Haverfordwest has for centuries been an important market town. There is a wide range of fresh local produce on sale here, along with locally made crafts and a popular open air Farmer's Market. There is also a large open air market held on Sundays on Withybush airfield.

THE OLD SMITHY

Established by Janet and Dario Algieri in 1998, The Old Smithy at Simspon Cross has been much improved and expanded. It now has 3 large display areas including a well lit and presented gallery showing original work by many local artists, plus prints and cards. The other 2 rooms have a wide selection of Welsh inspired and sourced crafts and gifts including; wooden bowls, vases etc by resident woodturner (who is often on site), plus slate coasters and placements. Celtic jewellery, glass ornaments, Caldey Island perfumes and chocolate. Organic soaps and oils, fudge and biscuits from Daffodil Cottage, Gwynedd Confectionery, Welsh Dolls and fluffy dragons, slippers and other sheepswool products, Welsh books and much more.

THE WEST COAST

HAVERFORDWEST TOURISM

Visitors can enjoy a day at Broad Haven with its wide sweep of golden sand and near unrivalled record for safe bathing or, virtually alongside, the smaller village of Little Haven.

Dale and Marloes are interesting villages and both are en route to some of the most famous bird sanctuary islands in Europe - Skomer and Skokholm, both of which teem with an unbelievable variety of seabirds. Information about trips can be obtained from Tourist Information 01437 763110. Embarcation for the islands is at St Martin's Haven, through the village or Marloes. Trips around the islands, enjoying the spectacular coastline are particularly recommended. In the early autumn there are opportunities to see the hundreds of Atlantic Grey Seals which come ashore to give birth.

North of the county the scenery becomes more rugged. Britain's smallest city, St David's, with its wonderful cathedral nestling in a picturesque valley, built there to protect it from Norse invaders and nearby is the golden Whitesands Bay.

On the way to St David's visitors pass the long beach of Newgale, protected by its high bank of pebbles, an ideal place to for surfing. From Newgale the road splits and visitors face the quandary of travelling through the small peaceful cove of Nolton Haven to Broad Haven or through Newgale where the road later drops down into the village of Solva with its picturesque inlet and gaily coloured yachts and flotilla of boats.

Haverfordwest is ideally located to explore Britain's only coastal National Park.

The magnificent coastline can be seen at its best from the Coast Path, a designated National Trail, stretching 186 miles from Amroth in the south to St Dogmael`s in the north. As with any rugged landscape the walker needs to be fully prepared to enjoy this challenging path in safety. The entire route represents an impressive physical challenge, including 25,000 feet of ascent and decent. However it also offers a tremendous variety of shorter day walks with the possibility of the Puffin Shuttle bus service to aid the tired walker.

It is Britain's most westerly National Park and one of the most precious environmental areas in Europe. It is famous for its seal and seabird colonies and the wild flowers, which flourish in the mild climate. The Pembrokeshire Coast National Park Authority cares for this special area and one of their aims is to help visitors and locals to enjoy what the park has to offer.

SCOLTON HERITAGE PARK

Within the park's 60 acres of landscaped grounds and woodland stands Scolton House, which dates back to the 1840's and is furnished throughout in the style of the 1920's. New displays in the Victorian stable block illustrate what life was like on a Pembrokeshire country estate, including stabling, cart shed, carpenter's workshop and smithy. Other attractions include an animal enclosure, arboretum, nature trail and a new "green" visitor centre made entirely of local materials.

for more information ring 01437 731328

RHOS

Virtually on the doorstep of this quiet and attractive little village, situated about two miles to the south of the main A40 Haverfordwest to St.Clears road, is the stately Picton Castle. The road through the village also gives you access to the banks of the Eastern Cleddau, an ideal picnic site on a warm Summer's day. Facing you across the water here is the slipway at Landshipping and a few hundred yards to your right is Picton Point, the confluence of the Western and Eastern Cleddau rivers.

LITTLE HAVEN

This is a tiny village resort of great charm and beauty, nestling between high cliffs. The beach, a sandy cove which at low tide connects with neighbouring Broad Haven, is popular with bathers and boaters and visitors to its welcoming pubs and restaurants. It is hard to imagine that coal from local pits was once exported from here.

Little Haven

Broad Haven

BROAD HAVEN

A favourite beach for bathers since 1800, Broad Haven is the biggest and the most popular resort on Pembrokeshire's west coast. The village has good facilities, including a cafe, guesthouses, shops, watersports equipment hire, public toilets and plenty of self catering accommodation, from caravans to cottages. At the Northern end of the superb long sandy beach are a number of interesting geological features - folding stacks and natural arches.

Broad Haven

WOLF'S CASTLE

Wolf's Castle (also frequently referred to in print as Wolfscastle) is at the northern end of the Treffgarne Gorge, where, in the early part of the century, railwaymen toiled to blast an unlikely route through the very old and very hard rock bed in a bid to fulfil Brunel's dream. A motte and bailey castle stands near the centre of the village, which is popular with holidaymakers by virtue of its inn, hotel and pottery. Archaeological finds nearby include Roman tiles and slates, indicating the site of a fortified Roman-British villa. The village was the birthplace in 1773 of Joseph Harris, who in 1814 published Seren Gomer, the first all Welsh weekly newspaper.

ROCH

Dominating the otherwise flat landscape for miles around, Roch Castle stands on an igneous rock outcrop. The origin of the castle and its large pele tower is unknown, but it is thought that it was built in the 13th century by Adam de Rupe. Legend says that he chose the site because of a prophecy that he would die from an adder's bite. Unluckily for him, an adder was brought into the castle in a bundle of firewood and duly fulfilled the prediction.The small village of Roch has a 19th century church with a circular churchyard.

NEWGALE

A popular surfing resort, newgale is a small village at the north-eastern end of St. Bride's Bay, overlooking the impressive two mile stretch of Newgale Sands. The sands are separated from the road and village by a high ridge of pebbles. At exceptionally low tides the stumps of a drowned prehistoric forest are sometimes exposed.

TREFFGARNE

Treffgarne was the birthplace of the rebellious Welsh hero Owain Glyndwr. The village stands close to the wooded rocky gorge, through which runs the Western Cleddau river, railway line and main A40 trunk road. The Treffgarne Gorge was cut by meltwater rushing south towards Milford Haven during the retreat of the last Ice Age. The areas around the gorge are dotted with sites of early settlements and fortifications, and on the western side rises the igneous outcrop of Great Treffgarne Mountain and other striking rock formations.

NANT-Y-COY MILL

Restored Nant y Coy Mill dates back to 1332 and possibly even earlier. The last corn was ground here in the 1950's, but the mill wheel is still turning 150 years after it was built. With a nature trail leading up to the Great Treffgarne Rocks, from where the views of the gorge are spectacular. You can also take a detour to Lion Rock and Bear Rock, two of the most distinctive features of the Pembrokeshire landscape.

NOLTON HAVEN

This compact coastal village, with its attractive cove, is virtually midway between little Haven and Newgale. In the 18th century, coal was exported from here, and the the line of the tramway which brought the anthracite and coal from the mines to the coast can still be seen. Alongside the old track bed is the Counting House, which recorded how many wagonloads of coal were transported to the quay. The quay itself, built in 1769, no longer exists. Half a mile north of Nolton Haven was Trefran Cliff Colliery, which worked coal seams beneath St. Bride's Bay between 1850 and 1905. Part of an old chimney and other ruins are now the only evidence of this once thriving industry.

Nolton Haven

Newgale

Milford Haven

RUDBAXTON

Rudbaxton is about 2 miles north of Haverfordwest and is the site of one of the region's most impressive earthworks, a motte and bailey fortress established in the 11th century. In a valley below the mound is the parish church of St. Michael. This dates from the 12th century and was restored in the 1870's.

MILFORD HAVEN

DISTANCES: Fishguard 24m, Haverfordwest 7m, Narberth 15m, Pembroke 7m, St. Davids 21m, Tenby 17m, Carmarthen 37m and London 253m

Since its development as a new town and whaling port in the late 18th century, Milford Haven has seen its economic fortunes seesaw. Sir William Hamilton, husband of Nelson's Emma, was granted an Act of Parliament to proceed with the development of the town and port, and from the beginning it was envisaged that new Milford would secure its share of the transatlantic shipping trade. Assisted by settlers from overseas, progress was rapid, with the early establishment of a quay, custom house, inn and naval dockyard. When Nelson visited in 1802 he was suitably impressed with the development and the Haven waterway, which he described as "one of the worlds finest natural harbours".During the mid 1800's, a renewed effort was made to re-establish Milford Haven as a transatlantic staging post, and ambitious plans were drawn up for the building of docks to rival those at Liverpool and Southampton. Although these never materialised, the far more modest Milford Haven docks opened in 1888. New life was breathed into the new docks, when the first vessel to enter was the steam trawler Sybil on the 27th September 1888. Her arrival marked the beginning of a prosperous new era for Milford Haven as the port turned its attention to deep-sea fishing.

The combination of new docks, excellent fishing grounds and good rail links saw the enterprise reap rich rewards. In its heyday in the 1920's, the port was home to 130 deep sea trawlers which offered employment to around 4, 000 men either afloat or ashore. By the 1950's the seesaw had tipped the other way again as the fishing industry slipped into an irretrievable decline. This time however, the promise of yet another new beginning for Milford Haven was already in the pipeline, the coming of the oil industry. In recent years this industry too has had its ups and downs. Despite the industry's problems the wealth generated by oil has helped fund Milford Haven's massive new investment in tourism. This has seen the complete refurbishment of the old docks and the creation of the superb 150 berth marina. Many of the old buildings have been demolished, while others of historic significance have been renovated and now house such attractions as the museum. A thriving retail and business park has been developed which has attracted many new business to the docks area.

Milford Haven

It's all at **Milford Marina...**

on the quayside you'll discover Phoenix Bowl and Pirate Pete's Adventure Play, Milford Haven Museum and the many waterside shops, cafes, restaurants and galleries.

It also makes a fantastic vantage point for viewing the increasing number of cruise ships visiting Milford Haven Port and watching the hundreds of passengers coming ashore eager to explore the history and culture of Pembrokeshire.

The Marina itself provides the highest levels of customer service for bertholders, in a relaxed and friendly atmosphere combined with first class facilities.

Marina Control, Cleddau House,
Milford Marina, Milford Haven, Pembrokeshire SA73 3AF

- e enquiries@milfordmarina.com
- w www.milfordmarina.com
- @mh_waterway
- Milford Haven Waterway

The Yacht Harbour Association Ltd

Milford Marina

MILFORD HAVEN HERITAGE & MARITIME MUSEUM

OPENING TIMES
March- October
Mon - Sat: 10.30 - 16.00

ADMISSION FEES:
Adults £3.00
Concession: £2.00
Special arrangements can be made for group visits

CONTACT
The Old Customs House
Milford Marina, Milford Haven
SA73 3AF
Tel: 01646 694496
Email: milfordmuseum@gmail.com
www.milfordhavenmuseum.co.uk

Follow Us On twitter | Like us on Facebook

Milford Haven is an unusual town, developed by Quaker Whalers from New England. In the late 19th Century, a dock system was built in the hope of breaking into the Transatlantic Liner Trade. The home of a major fishing industry. As the fishing industry declined in the 1950's, its place was taken by the oil industry. The museum tells this historical story with models, artifacts, sound and pictures.

Photographs courtesy of Pembrokeshire Photography

NEYLAND

Neyland

Like Milford Haven, Neyland has been revitalised by the building of an impressive new marina and waterfront development, Brunel Quay. Its name could only be a reference to the great railway engineer, whose aim was to establish Neyland as a prosperous transatlantic port by choosing it as the terminus of the South Wales Railway. An impressive statue of Brunel in recognition of his achievements was unfortunately stolen, but plans are afoot for a replacement. At one time or another during the 18th and 19th centuries, virtually every port and resort on the entire Welsh coast had designs on winning the battle for the highly lucrative transatlantic trade. In that year the service was transferred to Fishguard in the north of the county. The railway remained operational until 1964 when the town's depot was closed.The route of the old railway line now provides an enjoyable country walk between the marina and the village of Rosemarket. Mountain bikers can also tackle the 14m circular Brunel Cycle Route.

DALE

This one time shipbuilding and trading port is now one of the most popular sailing centres in Pembrokeshire and has good facilities for visitors. Races are held on most days during the summer and in August there is a regatta. Close to the village is Dale Fort, one of the Victorian defences built to protect the waterway and is now used as a geographical field study centre. At the western end of the village, the road leads to the magnificent St Ann's Head, with its lighthouse and coastguard station from where there are stunning views of the Haven waterway and its busy shipping lanes.

MARLOES

This pretty little village with its attractive cottages and church lies en-route to Marloes Sands, off the B4327. Marloes Sands can be reached from the village or from Dale. The panoramic views above the beach take in the islands of Skomer, Skokholm and the much smaller Grassholm, which at low tide can be reached from the northern end of the beach. The road through Marloes village also gives you access to the peaceful cove of Martin's Haven, the departure point for Skomer Island and other island boat trips.

Marloes

SPORT & LEISURE

Health and fitness are increasingly important facets of modern lifestyles, and this is reflected in the growing number of visitors who come in great numbers to Pembrokeshire in search of sporting and activity holidays. Certainly there is no better place to choose, with the only coastline in Britain designated a National Park, Pembrokeshire combines the best of the great outdoors with the very best in indoor leisure facilities.

Activity Centres

BASE CAMP OUTDOOR CENTRE
Llawhaden, Narberth
Offers canoeing and kayaking, climbing and abseiling, walking and hillwalking.
tel: 01437 541318

CELTIC DIVING
The Parrog, Goodwick
Offers diving, snorkelling courses, refresher dives and boat trips.
tel: 01348 871938

DIVE PEMBROKESHIRE
Gelli Cottage
Ludchurch
Narberth
SA67 8LE
tel: 07545967180

FFOREST OUTDOOR
Bridge Warehouse, Teifi Wharf, Cardigan,
SA43 3AA
Clothing and accessories for a range of outdoor sports
including climbing, walking, kayaking and canoeing
tel: 01239 62 36 33
www.fforestoutdoor.co.uk

PEMBROKESHIRE DIVE CHARTERS
Heddfan,
Blockett Lane
Little Haven
SA62 3UH
tel:01646 602942
01437 781569

PEMBROKESHIRE WATER SPORTS
Ahoy Pembrokeshire,
15 Church Road,
Hazelbeach,
Milford Haven
SA73 1EB
tel:0845 427 5608
or Mobile: 07791 905 954

THE PRINCE'S TRUST
Pembrokeshire Adventure Centre
Cleddau Reach
Pembroke Dock
SA72 6UJ
tel: 01646 622013

WEST WALES WIND, SURF AND SAILING
Dale
Canoeing, kayaking, surfing, sailing, windsurfing and powerboats. Caters for wheelchair users
tel: 01646 636642

Puffins

BIRDWATCHING

Ardent twitchers or those who just enjoy watching birds can have the time of their lives whatever the season. In winter the rivers Teifi, Cleddau and Nevern are home to Little Egrets, Slovonian Grebes and Great Northern Divers, together with Wildfowl Waders. Spring sees the arrival of swallows, warblers and many varieties of seabirds, while inland Peregrine falcons, Merlins, together with Lapwings, Golden Plovers and Buzzards take to the sky. The islands of Ramsey, Skomer and Grassholm offer the widest selection of birds including Fulmars, Kittiwakes, Guillemots, Razorbills and Puffins to name but a few. Skomer has the distinction of being home to the largest colony of Manx Shearwaters in the world, while Grassholm has the second largest colony of Gannets in the North Atlantic. Elegug Stacks near Castlemartin also has large colonies of Guillemots, Razorbills and Kittiwakes, while the Welsh Wildlife Centre at Cilgerran near Cardigan is home to countless varieties of birds and wildfowl. Both Skomer and Ramsey can be visited by boat. Skomer boats run daily (except Mondays, excluding Bank Holidays) from Martins Haven between April 1st or Easter, which ever is sooner, until October 31st.

Contact Dale Sailing Company tel: 01646 603123/603110 There are a number of boat operators who visit Ramsey, contact Voyages of Discovery on 0800 854367 and 01437 721911 or Thousand Islands on 01437 721721, or pick up leaflets locally.

A number of the boat operators also visit Grassholm, where you can't go ashore. Vantage points for bird watching include Amroth, Strumble Head, Nevern Estuary, Cleddau Estuary, Carew Mill Pond, Fishguard Harbour, Westfield Pill at Neyland and Bosherston Lily Ponds near Pembroke.

CANOEING AND KAYAKING

North Pembrokeshire's dramatic coastline offers just the sort of conditions ideal for canoeing and kayaking. For beginners there are quiet sheltered bays where even the complete novice soon feels at home, while the more expert can take up the challenge of tide races and overfalls. Beginners are often surprised to discover that even on their first trip, under the guidance of an experienced and qualified instructor, they begin to master the basic skills and are able to enjoy the thrills of exploring cliffs and sea caves and negotiating rocks and waves.

TYF ADVENTURE
1, High Street, St. Davids.
tel: 01437 721611
freephone 0800 132588

PEMBROKESHIRE ADVENTURE CENTRE
Cleddau Reach
Pembroke Dock.
tel: 01646 622013
The Parrog, Fishguard.
tel: 01348 874803

FFOREST OUTDOOR
Bridge Warehouse, Teifi
Wharf, Cardigan,
SA43 3AA
tel: 01239 62 36 33
www.fforestoutdoor.co.uk

CLIMBING

Pembrokeshire offers climbers of all abilities the opportunity to experience some of the finest sea cliff climbing in the British Isles. The county's geographical location and mild winters mean all year round climbing on dry, warm rock, a treat rarely available in mountainous areas. So the area is very popular, especially during early bank holidays, and there may well be queues for some of the plum 3 star routes. The sea cliffs are the home of many nesting birds, some of them rare and because of this very necessary restrictions have been imposed in certain areas from early February until mid August. So climbers are advised to choose their routes carefully as it cannot be stressed too strongly that if climbers and wildlife are to co-exist successfully in this environmentally sensitive corner of Britain, the restrictions imposed must be adhered to. Further details of these restrictions are available from all National Park Information Centres and in the Climbers Guide to Pembrokeshire.

DAILY SURF REPORTS WHITESANDS
www.masimes.co.uk

NEWGALE
www.newsurf.co.uk

WILD WEST WALES
www.aswildasyouwantit.com

PEMBROKESHIRE
www.surfwithus.co.uk
www.pembrokeshireactive.co.uk

BROAD HAVEN
www.outerreefsurfschool.com
www.havensports.co.uk

PEMBROKESHIRE WATER ACTIVITIES
www.princes-trust.org.uk/adventure
www.touristnetuk.com
www.pembrokeshire-wales.info
www.pembrokeshirewatersports.co.uk
www.pembrokeshire-sports.co.uk
www.dive-pembrokeshire.com
www.activitywales.com

EQUIPMENT HIRE
www.pembrokeshireboatcharters.com
www.havensports.co.uk
www.tenbymarine.co.uk
www.surfdale.co.uk
www.masimes.co.uk

COURSES
www.outerreefsurfschool.com
www.whitesandssurfschool.co.uk
www.tyf.com
www.celticdiving.co.uk

FFOREST OUTDOOR
Bridge Warehouse, Teifi Wharf,
Cardigan, SA43 3AA
tel: 01239 62 36 33
www.fforestoutdoor.co.uk

Fforest Outdoor has West Wales' largest selection of equipment, clothing and accessories for a range of outdoor sports including climbing, walking, kayaking and canoeing, with over 35 boats of all shapes and sizes in stock. From our waterside location you can try before you buy on our entire range, book on a variety of activities, hire a mountain bike or just take a quiet coffee and cake in our dedicated adventure café! Find us by the old bridge in the centre of Cardigan.

CYCLING AND MOUNTAIN BIKING

There is no better way to enjoy the magnificence of the Pembrokeshire coastline and the beauty and tranquillity of the countryside than on a bike, especially as the whole of the National Park is crisscrossed with a network of hidden tracks, bridle ways and sunken lanes. When cycling in Pembrokeshire it is very important to remember that the coast path is for walkers only, a law strictly enforced by the National Park Authority, who are responsible for maintaining this long distance footpath. Furthermore, off road cyclists should give way at all times to walkers and horse riders, and be courteous and considerate to the farmers and landowners whose land they are crossing. For cyclists who prefer to be on the road than off it Pembrokeshire has more quiet lanes than most people could cycle round in a lifetime. Touring in the county could hardly be easier, with bed and breakfast available round every corner and plenty of youth hostels within easy reach.

COASTEERING

Another growing sport is Coasteering, which is definitely an activity for the more daring. It involves a combination of climbing and scrambling along the rocky coastline, swimming and cliff jumping into the sea.

DIVING

The natural beauty of Pembrokeshire with its picturesque countryside and dramatic scenery is mirrored in its underwater landscape. Diving is a very popular pastime with clubs from all over Britain visiting the clear water where hundreds of wrecks abound, and reefs offer a variety of fish life. Some of the dive sites are marine reserves so their inhabitants remain untouched. Seals often accompany divers as they explore the underwater world and if you're lucky enough, dolphins, porpoises and even sea horses have been known to swim in certain areas, particularly around Cardigan Bay where a pod of dolphins are resident to the area. There are dive sites to suit all abilities, from novice to the more experienced diver.

DIVE PEMBROKESHIRE
11 Meadow Park
Burton
Milford Haven
SA73 1N2
tel: 01646 600200

WEST WALES DIVING CENTRE
42 Sandyke Rd, Broadhaven
Haverfordwest, SA62 3JF
tel: 01437 781457

WEST WALES DIVING SCHOOL
Sessions Hall, Mathry
near Haverfordwest
tel/fax: 01348 831526

CELTIC DIVING BASE
The Parrog
Goodwick, Dyfed SA64 0DE
tel: 01348 871 938

FISHING

Whether you are looking for an out and out fishing holiday or you simply want to enjoy a bit of fishing while you're here, Pembrokeshire and West Wales provide wonderful opportunities for sea, game and coarse fishing. The coastlines of Pembrokeshire, Cardigan Bay and Carmarthen Bay are excellent venues for summer sea angling, either from the beach or from established rock marks. Bass, pollack, garfish, mackerel, conger eel and even tope are all here for the taking, while if you want to fish offshore, there is no shortage of charter boats offering fishing trips from local harbours. West Wales has long been renowned for the quality of its game fishing, with most of the area's rivers and their tributaries experiencing good runs of salmon and sea trout during the summer months. Indeed, the region boasts three of Britain's premier salmon rivers, the Towy, Teifi and Taf, and many others provide terrific sport when conditions are favourable. These include the Nevern, Aeron, Eastern Cleddau, Western Cleddau, Rheidol and Ystwyth. Wales also has an abundance of lakes and reservoirs that are well stocked with brown and rainbow trout. Venues popular with visitors are the reservoirs at Llys-y-fran Country Park and Rosebush, both close to the B4329 about six miles from Haverfordwest, White House Mill and Latch y Goroff, (near Whitland) and the fisheries of Llwyndrissi, Llanllawddog and Garnffrwd, (near Carmarthen). For coarse anglers there are exciting prospects at a variety of locations. Bosherston Lakes offer excellent pike fishing and Llyn Carfan Lake at Tavernspite boasts top class carp fishing and a good head of tench and roach. Glas Llyn fishery near Blaenwaen is also stoked with carp and tench. But remember, anyone over 12 years old who fishes for salmon, trout, freshwater fish or eels in England and Wales must have an Environmental Agency rod fishing licence, available from the Post Office or Environment Agency offices. In addition, you must have permission from the fishery owner before you may fish on waters under their control, and remember to take your litter home, as discarded tackle can injure wildlife.

see advert page 149

Pembrokeshire Coast

NATIONAL PARK

The Pembrokeshire Coast National Park, one of Britain's breathing spaces, takes in about a third of the county including the entire coastal strip, the upper reaches of the Daugleddau (two swords) and the Preselis. It's the only National Park that is almost all coastal. The National Park run an extensive programme of activities and events for both adults and children: rockpool safaris, crab catching, bat walks and even time travel.

Britain's Only Coastal National Park.

It covers a third of Pembrokeshire including the Preseli Mountains and the upper reaches of the Daugleddau Estuary.

Tenby, St Davids, Saundersfoot, Newport and Manorbier are all in the National Park.

So are Skomer, Skokholm, Caldey and Ramsey Islands. Two inland areas are also in the National Park, The Preseli Mountains and the upper reaches of the Daugleddau Estuary.

The Preseli Mountains are where the Stonehenge bluestones are supposed to have come from.

The Daugleddau Estuary is known, locally, as the secret waterway.

WALKING ROUTES

The best known footpath is the Pembrokeshire Coast Path, which winds its way around the magnificent bays and spectacular headlands. The 186 mile, 299km trek is a strenuous undertaking if you want to complete the route from start to finish.

DINAS ISLAND is a rocky headland near Fishguard. Start at either Cwm yr Eglwys or Pwllgwaelod and take the coast path around the island, returning to your start point via the low lying valley that connects it to the mainland. Total distance covered is about 3 miles or 5km. Catch the Poppit Rocket the walker's bus.

CARREGWASTAD POINT Start in the pretty village of Llanwnda, near Fishguard and backtrack along the road for 1/4 mile before cutting across country towards the ferry terminal at Goodwick. Pick up the coast path and follow it round to Carregwastad Point. If you want to turn back here the distance is about 5 miles or 9km. To carry on to Strumble Head will double the distance. Catch the Strumble Shuttle the walker's bus.

CEMAES HEAD is a rugged and wild section of intensely folded high cliffs. Start at the car park at Poppit near St. Dogmael's and walk up the road past the Youth hostel. Follow the coast path to Ceibwr Bay, a distance of 5.5m/7km. By the time you've returned, across country, you'll have covered 9miles or 16km. Catch the Poppit Rocket the walker's bus.

From the National Park car park at MANORBIER BEACH, below the castle, two walks are available, one going west to the secluded Swanlake Bay a distance of 3miles/5km. The path to the east provides a short circular walk returning through the village. Local Bus Service 349/359

STRUMBLE HEAD is a wild and unpopulated stretch of the path with some spectacular cliffs. Start at the car park at Garn Fawr, 2 miles south of Strumble Head and follow winding country lanes all the way to Strumble lighthouse. Continue along the coast path to the Youth Hostel at Pwll Deri and return to the car park via the hilltop where you get magnificent views of the Pen Caer peninsula you've just walked around. Total distance 5miles, 9km. Catch the Strumble Shuttle the walker's bus.

Either start at ABEREIDDY or at PORTHGAIN, a safe—haven harbour with a good pub and restaurant. There's plenty of interest on the way includ—ing old stone quarries, the Blue Lagoon — a flooded slate quarry and the secret beach of Traeth Llyfn. Returning to your starting point via Barry Island Farm and Felindre House. Total distance is 4 miles/6km. Catch the Strumble Shuttle the walkers bus.

ST. DAVIDS PENINSULA Start behind the Cathedral and follow the lanes north along the valley. When you reach Treleddyd Fawr continue across country until you reach the coast path which you can then follow all the way round the peninsular to Caerfai before returning to St. Davids. This route cover 15miles, 23km or it can be tackled in smaller sections: Whitesands to St. Davids Head and back via Carn Llidi 4 miles/6km Porthstinian to Porthclais and return on the country roads 6miles/10km St. Davids to Porthclais and return via Caerfai 2miles/3km. Catch the Celtic Coaster the walker's bus (summertime only)

Thanks to the introduction of the PUFFIN SHUTTLE between St. Davids and Milford Haven, some excellent stretches of the coast path can now be tackled without the need to do a circular route. Use the shuttle to travel to the far end of your day's walk and walk back to where you started. Good sections to tackle in this fashion include: Solva to St Davids•Newgale to Solva•Little Haven to Nolton Haven•St Brides Haven to Little Haven •Dale to Martins Haven

Take a circular route around the MARLOES PENINSULA, starting at either Marloes beacon or the National Trust car park for Marloes beach. It covers a distance of 6.5miles/11km

Another good circular route is around the DALE PENINSULA, starting from the car park near St. Ann's head. The path follows some dramatic cliff tops, dropping down to several lovely sandy coves on the way. Total distance is about 6miles/10km.

SOUTH OF MILFORD HAVEN, another circular route is possible around the Angle Peninsula, starting from either Freshwater West or from West Angle Bay. Travelling in a clockwise direction, you are treated to one of the most dramatic views in Britain as you come over the ridge and see the magnificent beach at Freshwater West stretching away into the distance. Total distance is around 9miles/15km.

The coast path between STACK ROCKS and BROAD HAVEN SOUTH is only accessible when the army ranges are not firing. It's a fascinating stretch of coast but can't be easily incorporated into a circular route because the ranges get in the way. Some unusual rock features, arches, stacks, caves and hidden beaches as well as a visit to St. Govan's Chapel make the walk interesting. Distance one way is 4miles/7km. Catch the Coastal Cruiser bus

STACKPOLE QUAY is the start point for a good walk that takes in dramatic cliffs, the lily ponds at Bosherston and one of the most remarkably unspoilt beaches in Britain, Barafundle. As with the previous walk, there isn't a circular option, merely retrace your steps. With teashops at both ends, Stackpole Quay and Bosherston Village, dehydration shouldn't be a problem. Total distance 4miles/7km. Catch the Coastal Cruiser bus

The coast path from TENBY to SAUNDERSFOOT passes some of the best beaches you're likely to find in Britain including Glen beach, Monkstone and Waterwynch. There's a regular bus service between the towns, the best way to organise a circular route. To walk the route from one direction from harbour to harbour is around 4 miles/6km.
Local Bus Service 350/351

LLYS-Y-FRAN COUNTRY PARK.
Approximately 7.5 miles, 11km around the reservoir, focal point of the Country Park which has car parks on each side of the lake. Picnic sites, visitor centre, licensed restaurant, toilets, exhibitions area and shops available.Special events and guided walks are also arranged. These include a tour of the reservoir, woodland bird spotting, the chance to try fly fishing and children activities days (including a boat trip)
Tel: 01437 532273/532694 for details.

From SAUNDERSFOOT to AMROTH the coast path follows an old tramway, which takes in a series of tunnels for the first mile. The route there and back is approx 5 miles/8km. Local bus service 350/351

Walkers Coastal Bus Services
www.pembrokeshire.gov.uk/coastbus

Walking ideas
www.visitpembrokeshire.com/walking

Pembrokeshire Coast Path National Trail
www.visitpembrokeshire.com/coastpath

Pembrokeshire Coast National Park
www.pembrokeshirecoast.org.uk/walking

The Preseli Circle & Greenways walking holidays
www.greenwaysholidays.com

Beach wheelchair hire
www.pembrokeshire-access.org.uk

Catering for all the family

Pembrokeshire is a perfect holiday destination for you and your furry friend. With over 50 beaches and 186 miles of the Pembrokeshire Coastal path, there is always somewhere interesting for walkies!

Beaches with dog restrictions between 1st May & 30th September

Lydstep Haven – the western end of the beach
Newgale – between the two main car parks
Saundersfoot – between the harbour and The Strand
Tenby North Beach and The Harbour – all of it
Tenby Castle and South Beaches – from Castle Hill as far as South Beach car park
Amroth – all but the eastern end of the beach
Whitesands – the whole beach
Poppit – from the entrance to the car park directly north over the dunes and beach
Dale – from the car park to the rocks away from the village
Broad Haven (St Brides Bay)-The northern half of the beach

Golf Courses

DERLLYS COURT GOLF CLUB

A delightful 18 hole treelined course of parkland nature, set in beautiful Carmarthenshire countryside with easy access off the bypass between Carmarthen and St. Clears.

for more information
tel: 01267 211575

TENBY GOLF CLUB

Tenby hosts the oldest golf club in Wales where the Burrows offers a superb 18 hole links course. Overlooking Caldey Island, the clubhouse has a restaurant together with bar, lounge and snooker room.

tel: 01834 842978

TREFLOYNE GOLF COURSE

Trefloyne is a family owned golf course, located in the small village of Penally just outside Tenby. Trefloyne offers guests an 18 hole challenging parkland course set in mixed woodlands.

visit us at www.trefloyne.com

ST. DAVIDS CITY GOLF CLUB

Established in 1902, this is one of the oldest golf clubs in Wales, and certainly the most westerly. The all weather links course is playable all year round.

for more information ring the clubhouse
tel: 01437 721751

SOUTH PEMBROKESHIRE GOLF CLUB

This 18 hole hillside course is located at Pembroke Dock, on an elevated site overlooking the River Cleddau and the beautiful Haven Waterway.

for more information
call tel: 01646 621453

MILFORD HAVEN GOLF CLUB

A superb 18 hole par 71 meadowland course, with panoramic views of the Haven Waterway.

tel: 01646 697762

PRISKILLY FOREST GOLF CLUB

Priskilly Forest near Letterston is a nine hole course set in mature parkland and only a ten minute drive from the Stena Ferry terminal at Fishguard.

tel: 01348 840276

ROSEMARKET GOLF COURSE

Rosemarket offers a challenging and very long nine hole parkland course cursed with numerous sand and water hazards to test players.

HEATHERTON & HERONS BROOK GOLF COURSES

Other golf courses include one at St. Florence, an 18 hole pitch and putt course situated at the Heatherton Sports Park, tel: 01646 651025, and the 18 and 9 hole courses at the Heron's Brook Golf and Fishing Retreat in Narberth

tel: 01834 869209

NEWPORT GOLF CLUB

Newport Golf Club & Dormy House Holiday Flats: here you have a golf course which overlooks the magnificent coastline of Newport Bay. The clubhouse offers full catering facilities, and accommodation.

tel: 01239 820244
or visit
www.newportlinks.co.uk

SPORT & LEISURE ACTIVITIES

MARROS RIDING CENTRE
MARROS, PENDINE
CARMARTHENSHIRE
E-mail: info@marros-farm.co.uk

Marros Riding Centre is a family owned & run establishment providing horse riding & livery services to members of the public. At Marros we cater for all levels of riders from people who have never even seen a horse close up to the more experienced of riders.

We are located on the Pembrokeshire/Carmarthenshire border between Amroth and Pendine on the Coast road.

All staff have BHS and/or ABRS qualifications. All trek leaders have BHS Riding and Road Safety Certificates and are first aid trained. First aid kits and mobile phones are taken on all rides leaving the yard.

We take both individuals and families for treks along our woodland tracks.

For the more experienced rider we offer riding along the beach which is within easy reach of the centre.

We provide lessons for all levels of rider from complete beginners up to very experienced riders wanting to improve their skills.

We offer younger people the opportunity to own a pony for the day, learning what it is like to own a pony from all aspects (and I do mean all aspects, front & rear).

Please get in touch if you have any questions concerning anything on this site or if you want to make a booking for any activity.

If you want to make a booking within the next 7 days please phone and either speak to a member of staff or leave a message on the answer phone for someone to phone back - 01994 453777. E-mail is not our quickest method of getting in touch as we spend more time on the yard than in the office but we will get in touch as soon as possible.

KARTING

WEST WALES KARTING
Withybush Rd,
Haverfordwest SA62 4BW
Tel:01437 769555

CAREW KARTING
Carew Airfield,
Sageston, Nr Tenby
tel: 07974 540689
01559 384078
see advert page 103

QUAD BIKING

RITEC VALLEY BUGGIES
Penally, Nr Tenby
tel: 01834 843390
see advert on page 25

SAILING

Traditionally, dinghy sailing is very popular all over Pembrokeshire and southwest Wales. Yacht clubs such as Newport, Fishguard and Solva in the north of the county and Tenby and Saundersfoot in the South, offer a friendly club atmosphere and a variety of facilities and racing programmes. Along the Milford Haven waterway, perhaps the most popular sailing location because it is sheltered from the open sea, you will find some of the larger and more active clubs, such as Neyland, Pembroke Haven Pembrokeshire (Gelliswick, Milford Haven) and Dale. For yachtsmen, the Haven has 22 miles of navigable inland waterway, with the additional challenge of exciting offshore to the nearby islands of Skomer, Skokholm and Grassholm. There are marinas at Milford Haven and Neyland, pontoons at Dale, Angle, Burton and Neyland and various mooring sites all along the waterway.

DALE YACHT CLUB
tel: 01646 636362

MILFORD MARINA
tel: 01646 696 312

NEYLAND MARINA
tel: 01646 601601

PEMBROKESHIRE YACHT CLUB
Gelliswick,
Milford Haven
tel:01646 692799

Saundersfoot

Solva

PEMBROKESHIRE CRUISING
Neyland Marina,
Brunel Quay, Neyland
tel: 01646 602500

PEMBROKESHIRE WATERSPORTS
Ahoy Pembrokeshire,
15 Church Road,
Hazelbeach,
Milford Haven
SA73 1EB
tel: 0845 427 5608
or
Mobile: 07791 905 954

SOLVA SAILBOATS
1, Maes-y-Forwen
Solva, Haverfordwest
SA62 6TR
tel: 01437 720972

WEST WALES WIND, SURF &SAILING
Dale Sailing Company,
Brunel Quay, Neyland,
Milford Haven, SA73 1PY
tel: 01646 636642

SURFING AND WINDSURFING

Big waves, clear blue unpolluted waters, no crowds and relatively mild air and water temperatures - the tempting combination which Pembrokshire offers to surfers who are willing to travel that bit further in order to stand out from the rest. Late summer and early autumn are particularly good times to take advantage of the county's superb beaches and surfing conditions. Freshwater West, in South Pembrokeshire boasts the biggest and most consistent waves in the whole of Wales, with a variety of breaks to choose from. However there are strong currents and no lifeguards, so beginners should not surf here. Other beaches worth checking out nearby include Broad Haven (south), Freshwater East and Manorbier. In North Pembrokeshire, good surfing can be enjoyed at Whitesands Bay, Newgale, Broad Haven and West Dale. Age is no barrier to windsurfing which attracts enthusiasts from 8 to 80. Some enjoy setting sail in light winds for a tranquil afternoon cruise, whilst others like to display their competitive streak by racing, and for the most adventurous there are the strong winds and wave jumping.

Another big attraction of windsurfing is that it's easy to learn, provided you have the right equipment and tuition. One of Britain's top windsurfing and sailing venues is Dale. Its mile wide bay promises superb sea sailing on flat water, with no strong tidal currents, and is ideal for beginners and experts alike. West Wales Windsurfing, Sailing and Canoeing, is based on Dale waterfront and is a specialist watersports centre approved by the Royal Yachting Association. The expert tuition available here caters for everyone, from beginner to advanced windsurfers. All equipment is provided including wet-suits and buoyancy aids, and every instructor holds a nationally recognised qualification. As for recommending the best beaches, Broad Haven, (St. Brides Bay) and Newgale are ideal for more experienced windsurfers, except in particularly calm conditions, where as beginners and intermediates will breeze along more easily at Tenby, Saundersfoot, Newport and Fishguard.

SURF SHOPS AND HIRE

HAVEN SPORTS
Broad Haven
tel: 01437 781354

MA SIME'S SURF HUT
St. Davids
tel: 01437 720433

NEWSURF
Newgale
tel: 01437 721398

TYF ADVENTURE
St. Davids
tel: 01437 721611

CYCLING ROUTES

Pembrokeshire is the perfect county to see from the comfort of a bicycle. Long flat coastal roads, fantastic scenery and views to be enjoyed at a slow and relaxed pace.

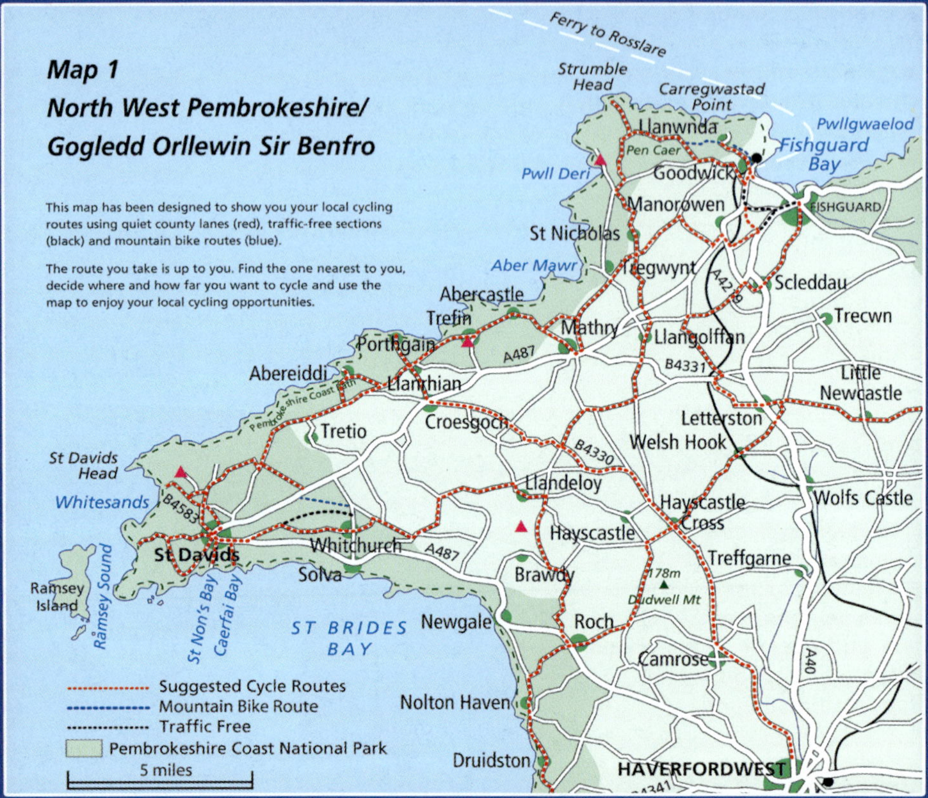

CYCLING INFORMATION

www.cyclepembrokeshire.com
www.sustrans.org.uk
www.cycle-n-sleep.co.uk
www.hiddentrails.com

CYCLING ROUTES

Pembrokeshire is the perfect county to see from the comfort of a bicycle. Long flat coastal roads, fantastic scenery and views to be enjoyed at a slow and relaxed pace.

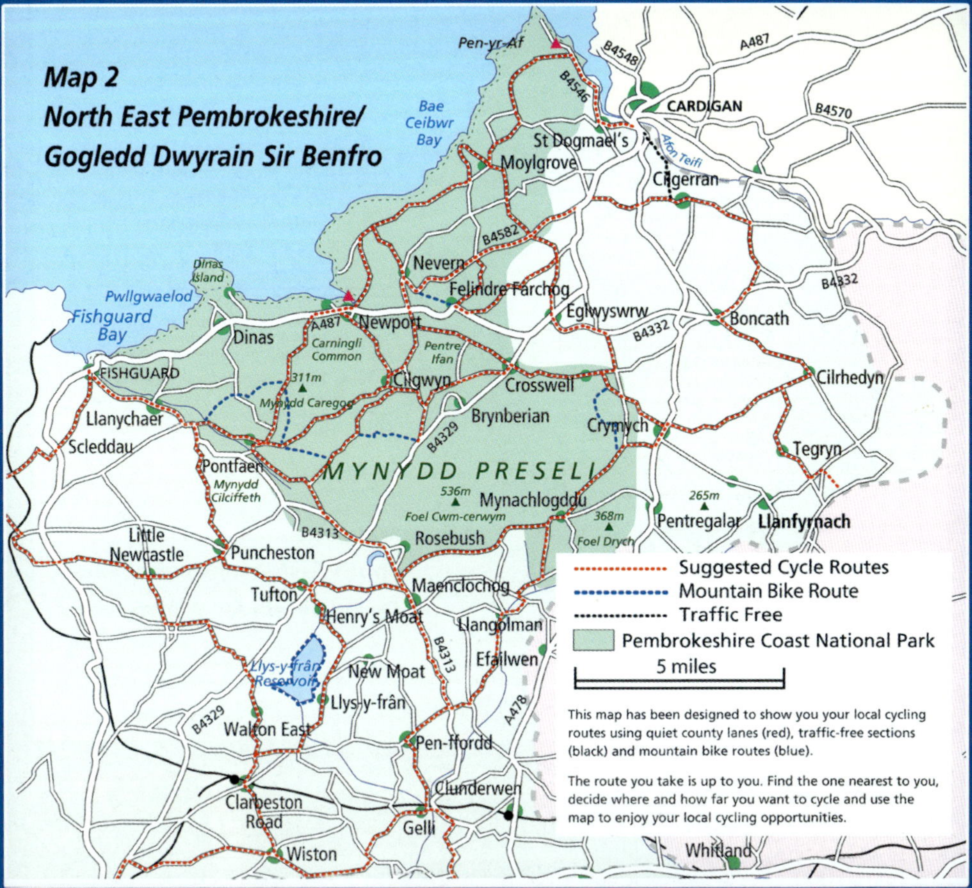

CYCLING INFORMATION

www.cycling.visitwales.com
www.pembrokeshireoutdoors.org.uk/cycling
www.pcnpa.org.uk
www.touristnetuk.com/Wa/PEMBS/activities/cycling

CYCLING ROUTES

Pembrokeshire is the perfect county to see from the comfort of a bicycle. Long flat coastal roads, fantastic scenery and views to be enjoyed at a slow and relaxed pace.

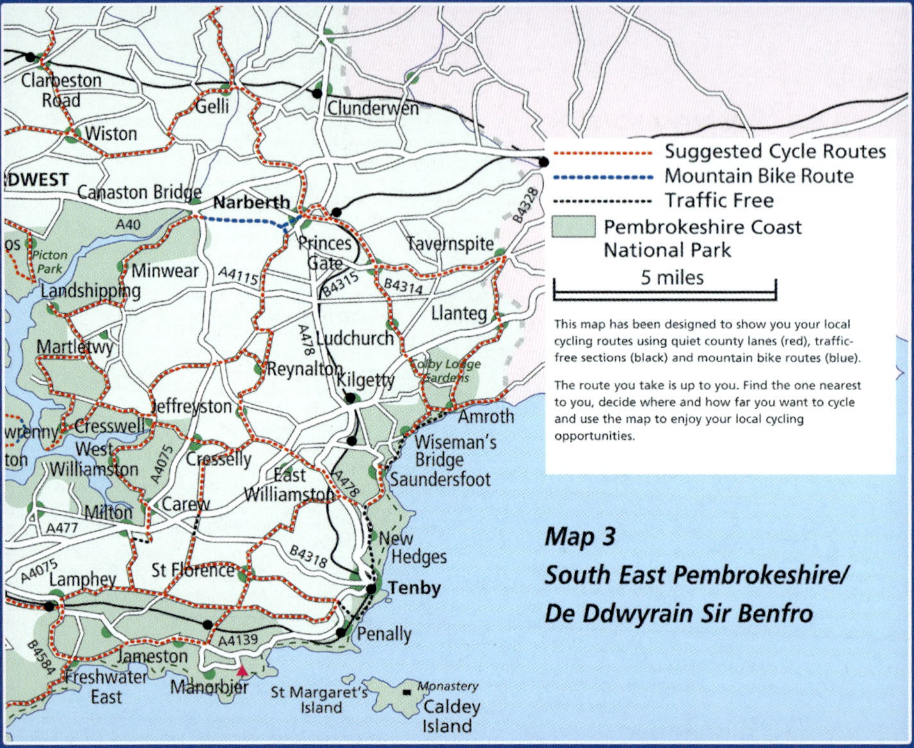

Map 3
South East Pembrokeshire/ De Ddwyrain Sir Benfro

CYCLING ROUTES

Pembrokeshire is the perfect county to see from the comfort of a bicycle. Long flat coastal roads, fantastic scenery and views to be enjoyed at a slow and relaxed pace.

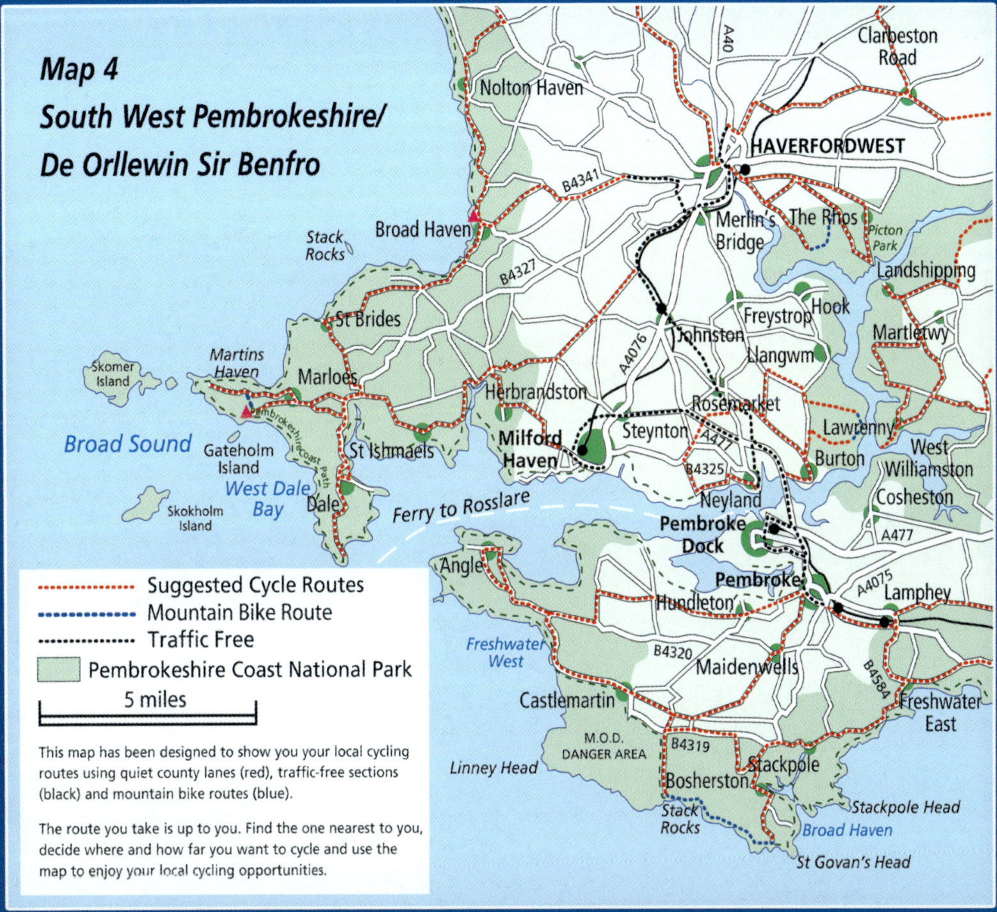

This map has been designed to show you your local cycling routes using quiet county lanes (red), traffic-free sections (black) and mountain bike routes (blue).

The route you take is up to you. Find the one nearest to you, decide where and how far you want to cycle and use the map to enjoy your local cycling opportunities.

CYCLING HOLIDAYS

www.greenwaysholidays.com
www.mayberryadventures.co.uk/Cycling.php
www.fbmholidays.co.uk/adventure_activities.aspx
www.activitywales.com

THE NORTH COAST

Compared with Tenby and the more developed South, North Pembrokeshire is better known for its rugged beauty and ancient landscape than its leisure attractions and amusements. Yet many of the features which annually bring hundreds of thousands of visitors to the area can be described truthfully as man made - some as long ago as 5000 years. The sights awaiting those visitors with a will to explore are as fascinating as they are varied.

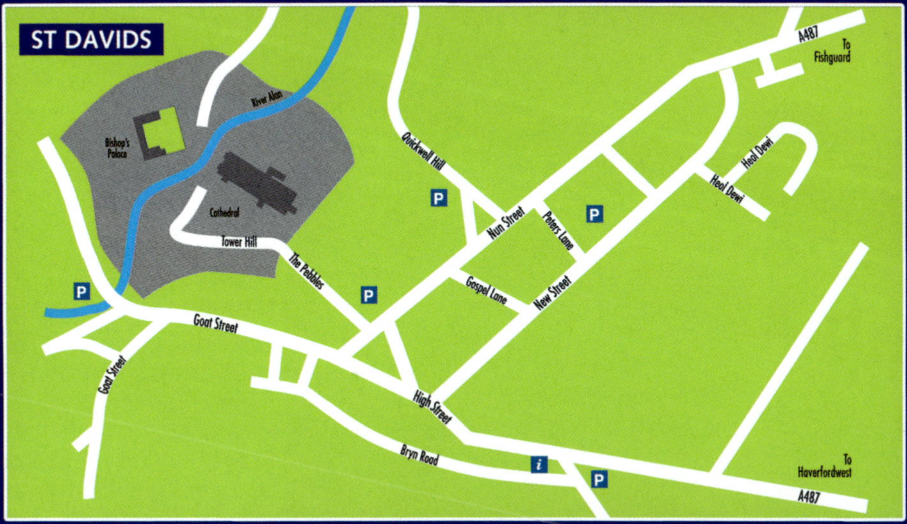

ST. DAVIDS

DISTANCES: Fishguard 16m Haverfordwest 16m, Milford Haven 21m, Narberth 25m, Pembroke 26m, Tenby 35m, Carmarthen 46m and London 266m

St. Davids is living proof that size is not important. As any visitor will quickly discover, the cathedral city is in reality a modest but very charming village. People still flock here in their thousands as they did throughout the Middle Ages when this was a place of pilgrimage, and the cathedral remains the major object of attention. Yet impressive and hugely significant though it is, the cathedral is small by English standards, and because it is hidden in a sheltered valley you could pass through St. Davids without even noticing that Wales' greatest religious monument is here. The village-cum-city dates back to the 6th century and stands about a mile from the sea, on a wide plateau overlooking the diminutive River Alun. The centre of St. Davids is marked by Cross Square so called because of its restored ancient cross. High Street is something of a misnomer, for the road runs in from Solva and Haverfordwest but does not contain City Hall. Inevitably all roads lead to the 12th century cathedral. Less well known, but no less impressive, are the ruins of the once magnificent Bishop's Palace, which stands opposite the cathedral in Cathedral Close. The close is an area of 18 acres, lying below the city in the vale of the River Alun. It is believed that this secluded site was chosen for the original 6th century church so that it would

Bishops Palace
Cross Square

not be visible from the sea to passing pirates and raiders, who frequently made it their business to ransack western coastal communities and pilfer whatever treasures the churches and chapels might contain. However, the ploy failed, Vikings burnt the church no less than eight times during the centuries leading up to the Norman Conquest. The path from the city down to Cathedral Close takes you through the 13th century Tower Gate, one of four gatehouses which formed part of the close's precinct wall. Within the Close stands the cathedral, the Bishop's Palace and various other ecclesiatical buildings, including the houses of church dignitaries. At this point you are still above the level of the cathedral and to reach it requires a further descent of a flight of thirty nine steps known as the Thirty-Nine Articles. The Cathedral and Bishop's Palace are marvels of medieval architecture, all the more striking for the remarkable tranquillity of this remote setting.

ST. DAVIDS CATHEDRAL

The cathedral as it stands today was begun in 1180 by Peter de Leia, the third Norman bishop, and completed in 1522. In 1220 the central tower collapsed, an occurrence apparently not unknown in medieval churches, and further damage was inflicted by a severe earthquake in 1248.

Early in the 14th century, Bishop Gower, nicknamed "The Building Bishop" because of his love of creating great buildings, carried out many changes and improvements to the cathedral. He raised the walls of the aisles, inserted the decorated and much larger windows, built the south porch and transept chapels and vaulted the Lady Chapel. In around 1340 he also built the Bishop's Palace to accommodate the large numbers of pilgrims visiting the cathedral. The Palace, a structure of such spendour that even the ruins are impressive, stands opposite the cathedral. As the cathedral expanded, an increasing number of clerical residences and other ecclesiastical buildings grew up around it, and a wall with gatehouses was built to protect the community. The last of the great builders to contribute to the cathedral was Bishop Vaughan, who in the early 16th century raised the tower to its present height and built the perpendicular chapel dedicated to the Holy Trinity. Following the Reformation the cathedral was neglected.

The roof was stripped of its lead and subsequently, though much later, collapsed. Severe damage was also inflicted in the Civil War. In 1862 Sir George Gilbert Scott was commissioned to begin a complete restoration of the cathedral, and not surprisingly the work continued into this century. In 1866, during the restoration, the bones of two men were found in a recess which had been walled up. It is believed that these were the remains of St. David and his friend and teacher St. Justinian. They are now contained in an oak chest in the Holy Trinity Chapel. Other tombs in the cathedral include those of Bishop Gower, Edmund Tudor, father of Henry VII, and Giraldus Cambrensis. St. Davids Cathedral which is open to visitors every day, is the largest church in Wales and is certainly the most interesting. The total interior length is nearly 300ft and the tower is 125ft high, small by comparison with cathedrals on the grand scale of York Minster, but a mighty inspiration to the Welsh for centuries past and, no doubt, for centuries to come

THE NORTH COAST

FRIDAY 27 MAY / DYDD GWENER 27 MAI
6.00pm Festival Launch
Sing Up! Sing Out!
The Festival opens with the Children's Festival Chorus directed by the inspirational voice coach and conductor Suzzie Vango. They will be accompanied by Ruairi Edwards (piano) and a live band: The Roar Tones. There will be music by Bob Chilcott, Rebecca Lawrence and Barry Manilow! Tickets £8 unreserved seating Children 16 and under, free This concert and the Festival's Educational Outreach programme are supported by the West Wales Masonic Grand Charity

SATURDAY 28 MAY / DYDD SADWRN 28 MAI
12.00 noon Cambrian Consort of Viols - 'In Nomine' Lunch time concert in the cathedral's North Transept. The Cambrian Consort of Viols with soprano Tabitha Rodway and directed by Father Paul Brophy perform 16th & 17th music by John Dowland, William Byrd, Orlando Gibbons and Thomas Tomkins (born in St Davids 1572).
Tickets £8 unreserved seating
Children 16 and under, half price

7.00pm BBC National Orchestra of Wales
Natalie Clein Cello Jessica Cottis Conductor Saint Saens Danse Macabre
Saint Saens Cello Concerto No. 1 in A minor
Tchaikovsky Symphony No. 6 in B minor (Pathetique)
One of the world's finest orchestras makes a welcome return to the Festival to perform a spectacular programme of 19th century masterpieces. Please book early to avoid disappointment
This concert will be recorded live by BBC Radio 3.
Tickets Reserved £25, £18, unreserved £10 Children 16 and under, half price

SUNDAY 29 MAY / DYDD SUL 29 MAI
7.30pm Haverfordwest Male Voice Choir - Music for a Summer Evening at Y Tabernacl, Goat Street, St Davids Richard Stephens Conductor Peter Griffiths Accompanist Don't miss the opportunity to hear this choir, part of the great Welsh tradition of male voice choirs, as they perform music by Robat Arwyn, Jacques Briel, Amanda Mc Broom and Eric Jones Tickets £12 unreserved seating Children 16 and under, free (NB There is no wheelchair access at this venue)

MONDAY 30 MAY / DYDD LLUN 30 MAI
10.30am Coffee Concert in the Education Centre, Ty'r Pererin A selection of music presented and performed by St Davids Cathedral Choral Scholars, Francis Shepherd (tenor) and James Bywater (bass).
Tickets £8 unreserved seating Children 16 and under, half-price The price of a ticket includes a cup of coffee

MONDAY 30 MAY / DYDD LLUN 30 MAI (continued)
2.00pm Family Concert – Prokofiev's Peter and the Wolf Michael Slaney Organ Jonathan Lean Narrator The cathedral's esteemed Assistant Organist Emeritus, Michael Slaney MBE is joined by the cathedral's Jonathan Lean to present this hour long concert, which includes the famous children's story and music written by the great Russian composer, Prokofiev.
Tickets £10, unreserved seating Children 16 and under, free

7.00pm Goodwick Brass Band
Matthew Jenkins Conductor
We are delighted to welcome to the Festival for the first time, the awardwinning Goodwick Brass Band for a rousing performance including music by Karl Jenkins and Philip Harper. Tickets £12 unreserved seating Children 16 and under, free

TUESDAY 31 MAY / DYDD MAWRTH 31 MAI
11.00am Young Organist Platform - Callum Alger For this year's concert we welcome to the cathedral's organ loft, Callum Alger, organ student at Birmingham Conservatoire and Director of Music at St Thomas' Church, Stourbridge. Tickets £8 unreserved Children 16 and under, free 7.00pm The Sixteen (Choral Pilgrimage) Harry Christophers After 35 years of recording and performing world-wide, The Sixteen is famous as one of the world's greatest choirs. They present this concert as part of their nationwide Choral Pilgrimage 2016. This spectacular concert will include music by William Byrd, Avro Pärt & Thomas Tallis. We expect this concert to sell out very quickly so please book early to avoid disappointment. Tickets £25, £18, unreserved £10 Children 16 and under, half-price

WEDNESDAY 1 June / DYDD MERCHER 1 MEHEFIN
10.30am Coffee Concert in the Education Centre, T 'r Pererin We welcome talented final year students Isabel Harries and Catherine Hare from London's Royal College of Music as they perform music written and arranged for Flute and Harp Duo. Tickets £8 unreserved Children 16 and under, half-price The price of a ticket includes a cup of coffee 8.00pm Sarah Gabriel with Galos Piano Trio Sarah Gabriel brings the renowned English composer and suffragette Dame Ethel Smyth's voice to life as she recounts her memories of the characters that inspired her time in Leipzig, the 'hotbed' of musical creativity. Music by Brahms, Grieg, Schumann and Ethel Smyth will be performed by the Galos Piano Trio. Tickets £15, £12 unreserved £8 Children 16 and under, free

THURSDAY 2 June / DYDD IAU 2 MEHEFIN
11.00am Live Music Now at Llanrhian Church Live Music Now offers activities to people of all ages whose access to live music is restricted due to special needs or challenging circumstancesTickets £10 unreserved Children 16 and under half-price. Wine and canapés will be available after this concert in Llanrhian Church Hall at a cost of £8

7.00pm A concert performance of the Opera - A Village at War
A moving story of love and courage in the face of adversity during WW1 told through the music and words of this renowned opera. Samuel Howley Composer Peter George Librettist The Synergy Chorus Seimon Morris Keyboard Menevia Orchestra Barry Haskey Leader Carol Mackintosh Director Tickets, £15, £12, unreserved £8 Children 16 and under, free

9.45pm Vox Angelica with St Davids Cathedral Vicars Choral & Choral Scholars
"Sing Joyfully" - For the first time, Vox Angelica and the Vicars Choral and Choral Scholars will be joining forces to perform a concert of music through the ages, including part songs, madrigals and songs from the shows.
Tickets £10 unreserved Children 16 and under, free

FRIDAY 3 June / DYDD GWENER 3 MEHEFIN
11.00am St Davids Cathedral Boys' Choir The Cathedral Boys' Choir are joined by the Vicars Choral & Choral Scholars to perform repertoire from the great British choral tradition. Tickets £8 unreserved Children 16 and under, free

7.00pm St Davids Cathedral Choir & British Sinfonietta
Simon Pearce continuo Oliver Waterer Conductor The Festival is delighted to welcome back the orchestra British Sinfonietta to join with the Cathedral Choir in this concert to cel brate Her Majesty the Queen's 90th birthday. The programme will include Handel's Coronation Anthems and music by Purcell. Tickets £22, £15, unreserved £8 Children 16 and under, half-price

Saturday 4 June / DYDD sadwrn 4 MEHEFIN
11.00am Young Musician of Dyfod This concert will be given in the North Transept by the winner of the annual Young Musician of Dyfed music competition, Tickets £8 unreserved Children 16 and under, free

7.00pm Festival Chorus and British Sinfonietta Haydn Insanae et vanae curae
Mozart Laudate Dominum Mozart Divertimento in D major Mozart Mass in C minor Oliver Waterer Conductor The Festival Chorus and soloists are joined for the first time by orchestra British Sinfonietta for the ever popular finale concert to the Festival. Tickets £22, £15 unreserved £8 Children 16 and under, half-price

Pembrokeshire Tourist Information Centres

www.visitpembrokeshire.com

TENBY TIC
Unit 2
Upper Park Road
Tenby
SA70 7LT
01834 842402
tenby.tic@pembrokeshire.gov.uk

PEMBROKE TIC
Pembroke Library&Information Centre
Commons Road
Pembroke
SA71 4EA
Tel: 01437 776499
Pembroke.tic@pembrokeshire.gov.uk

MILFORD HAVEN TIC
Suite 19
Cedar Court
Havens Head Business Park
SA73 3LS
Tel: 01437 771818
milford.tic@pembrokeshire.gov.uk

HAVERFORDWEST TIC
Former Youth Club
Off Dew Street
Haverfordwest
Pembrokeshire, SA61 1ST
Tel: 01437 775244
haverfordwestlendinglibrary@pembrokeshire.gov.uk

FISHGUARD TIC
The Town Hall
Market Square
Fishguard
SA65 9HE
01437 776636
fishguard.tic@pembrokeshire.gov.uk

PEMBROKESHIRE COAST NATIONAL PARK VISITOR CENTRES
www.pembrokeshirecoast.org.uk

ORIEL Y PARC
St Davids
SA62 6NW
01437 720392
orielyparc@pembrokeshirecoast.org.uk

NEWPORT TIC
2 Bank Cottages
Long Street
Newport
01239 820912

ST. NON'S CHAPEL

Non was the mother of David, the man destined to become the patron saint of Wales. Standing in a field above St. Non's Bay, just south of St. Davids, the original ruined chapel is reputedly the oldest Christian monument in Wales. It is also said to mark the exact spot where St. David was born in the 6th century, during a thunderstorm. Near the chapel is a holy well that miraculously appeared at the moment of birth. In the Middle Ages the well attracted many people who came to cure their ailments. The present St. Non's Chapel was built in 1934.

ST. JUSTINIAN'S

The name actually refers to the remains of St. Justinian's Chapel, but over time it has become synonymous with the little creek and harbour of Porthstinian. The presence of the chapel recalls the legend of St. Justinian, who founded a small religious community on nearby Ramsey Island. The discipline he imposed on his followers was so strict that they rebelled and cut off his head, whereupon St. Justinian picked it up, walked over the sea to the mainland, laid down on his head and died.

PORTHCLAIS

In centuries past, this picturesque inlet was a busy little harbour, the port of the monastic community at St. Davids. Its sheltered anchorage saw the comings and goings of countless monks, priests, pilgrims, Norman soldiers, pirates and even Kings. Purple stone from nearby Caerfai and Caerbwdy was landed here to help build the cathedral, along with Irish oak for the roof of the nave. Trade thrived here in the Tudor and Stuart periods, with exports of cereal to the West Country.

Porthclais

PORTHSTINIAN

Porthstinian is well known as the home of the St. Davids lifeboat station. This was founded in 1868, though it was 1912 before the building and slipway were built. The rocky coastline and dangerous offshore reefs, such as the Smalls and the Bishops and Clerks, make this an extremely treacherous area for seaborne traffic, and the lifeboats which have seen service here have been involved in many dramatic rescues.

Porthstinian

St Brides Bay Cottages

Nine Wells, Solva, SA62 6UH
Tel: 01437 720027 Email: enquiries@stbridesbaycottages.com
www.stbridesbaycottages.com

St Brides Bay Cottages offers delightful cottages in superb locations around St Davids, Solva and Porthgain, where the scenery is spectacular, the air is fresh, the villages are full of character and where there is always a warm welcome. Pembrokeshire is the perfect backdrop for a real get-away-from-it-all holiday.

No. of units: **26** | Open: **All year**
Rates: PUPW **£330-£2140**

Solva

SOLVA

Without question this must be one of the most charming and attractive coastal villages in Britain. Just east of St. Davids on the A487 Haverfordwest road, Solva is a beautiful rocky inlet which floods at low tide providing a sheltered, safe anchorage for yachts and pleasure craft. Not surprisingly, this fine natural harbour has given the village a long seafaring tradition Shipbuilding and maritime trade flourished here until the railway arrived in Pembrokeshire in the middle of the 19th century. In its heyday the busy port had a thriving import and export business, nine warehouses, twelve limekilns, a direct passenger service to New York and also played an important role in the construction of the two remote lighthouses erected at different times on the smalls, a treacherous cluster of jagged rocks lurking 21 miles off Pembrokeshire's west coast. The facts relating to the passenger service to New York are a particularly fascinating slice of Solva's history. In 1848 the one way fare for an adult was £3. For this you were sure of a bed space, but had to take your own food, and the voyage could take anything from 7 to 17 weeks. The most popular part of this favourite holiday village, which is split into two, is Lower Solva with its harbour, surviving limekilns and a charming selection of shops, pubs and restaurants. Solva is an excellent place to join the Pembrokeshire Coastal Path, as the cliff scenery on either side of the inlet is magnificent. If you fancy an easy stroll you can walk along the harbour or take the footpath above the opposite (eastern) side of the inlet. This takes you to the top of the Gribin - a strip of land between two valleys - where you can see the site of an Iron Age settlement and superb views of the village and harbour.

Solva

Abereiddy

MIDDLE MILL

Just north of Solva, a mile up the valley of the river of the same name, nestles the attractive little waterside hamlet of Middle Mill. Here you will find a working woollen mill, which opened in 1907 and has been in production ever since. This family run business invites you to watch the process that turns the finest Welsh wool into a range of high quality rugs, tweeds, carpets and clothes, all of which are for sale on the premises.

ABEREIDDY

An attractive west facing bay on the north coast of the St. Davids Peninsula, Abereiddy is famous locally for its striking Blue Lagoon once a slate quarry linked to the sea by a narrow channel, but closed in 1904 after it was flooded during a storm. The lagoon is now considered an important geological feature, and the quarry yields many fossils. The coastal scenery between here and St. Davids Head is outstanding. To the north there are traces of the old narrow gauge railway track which once took the quarried slate and shale to the harbour at nearby Porthgain for export. Abereiddy is about two miles east of Croesgoch, on the A487 St. Davids to Fishguard road.

The Blue Lagoon

PEMBROKESHIRE SHEEPDOGS

On the beautiful north coast of Pembrokeshire, close to St. Davids is Tremynydd Fach Farm, home of Pembrokeshire Sheepdogs Training Centre. The centre runs courses for owners, handlers and their dogs from novice right up to "One Man and His Dog" standard. However, for the casual visitor they also run demonstrations throughout the season, which allow everyone to watch a wonderful exhibition of the skills of the working dogs. From the youngest pups just beginning to show the natural instincts for their work, through all stages of training, to dogs of three or four years at the height of their skills. All can be seen working sheep, and other animals, and clearly having a great time doing it. There is also a surprise finale.Teas and home baked cakes at extremely reasonable prices, plus the opportunity to talk to the handlers, make this a wonderful insight into working dogs. You can even bring your own dog to watch but keep them on a lead please.

for further information call 01437 721677

Abereiddy

LLANRHIAN

Llanrhian is a hamlet standing at a crossroads on the road between Croesgoch and Porthgain. It is notable because of the unusual parish church, dedicated to St. Rhian, which is cruciform in shape, and has a number of interesting features including a 15th century ten sided font. Also striking is the tall tower, built in the 13th century. The rest of the church was completely rebuilt in 1836 and restored in 1891.

PORTHGAIN

A small hamlet in the parish of Llanrhian, Porthgain is one of the most individual places in Pembrokeshire, with superb coastal scenery and an unpretentious mixture of traditional, Victorian and later style houses and a man made 19th century harbour. The harbour was once a hive of activity and its reconstruction between 1902 and 1904 to make way for larger quays reflected its significant shipping activities. These included the exportation of slate and shale from the quarry at Abereiddy and bricks made from local clay, mainly for local use. The main export however was the medium to fine granite stone; exceptionally hard and used for the construction of buildings and roads as far apart as Liverpool, Dublin and London. Porthgain was a village whose employment was entirely dependant on the prosperity of the quarry and by the turn of the century, the company known as Porthgain Village Industries Ltd. boasted a fleet of nearly 100 vessels including six steam coasters of 350 tons each. Even as late as 1931, the harbour was improved for a hoped for 170ft 650 ton ship to enter, but after the First World War this maritime trade went into decline and by 1931 had ceased production entirely. In 1983 the Pembrokeshire Coast National Park Authority acquired the attractive harbour and the remains of the buildings bear testimony to Porthgain's industrial past. Porthgain remains a very lively community with a flourishing tourism trade due to its magnificent stretch of coastline and many significant antiquarian remains, making it a must see for those interested in either industrial archaeology or ancient history. A couple of miles north east of Porthgain lies a fine Iron Age fort called Castell Coch. Porthgain is well worth a visit for its diversity of interest. One of Britain's finest geographers described the coast between Porthgain and Abereiddy as the finest in Britain. Today fish are still regularly landed at Porthgain harbour. The Sloop Inn at Porthgain is probably one of the best known pubs in the area. The pub dates back to 1743, when it was more a workers than walkers pub. Nowadays, the Sloop makes a welcome stop for those walking along the coastal path. The premises offer good parking and space for children to play together with a large picnic area.

Porthgain

Porthgain

Trefin

MATHRY

The village of Mathry stands on a hill just off the A487 between St. Davids and Fishguard, a few miles east of Trefin. Its elevated position gives superb coastal views and of particular interest here is the parish church. This unusual squat building and circular churchyard occupy a prehistoric site, possibly dating from the Iron Age. At one time the church had a steeple that served as a landmark for mariners. Like Trefin, the village is a popular watering hole for visitors passing through. Just west of Mathry is the ancient site of a burial chamber.

TREFIN

Just to the east of Porthgain and its attractive harbour, Trefin is the largest coastal village between St. Davids and Fishguard. It is close to a shingle and sand beach known as Aber Felin and the proximity of the coast path makes this a popular watering hole for walkers. It is worth noting that disabled visitors can gain easy access to this section of the coast path. There is also a youth hostel in the village. Near the shoreline stands the ruin of Trefin Mill, which closed in 1918 and has been partly restored by the National Park Authority. The mill was immortalised in the famous Welsh poem, Melin Trefin.

Trefin

ABERCASTLE

Abercastle stands on Pembrokeshire's rocky northern coastline, southwest of Strumble Head and close to the villages of Trefin and Mathry. From the 16th century onwards this was a busy little coastal port, at various times in its history involved in the export of corn, butter and oats and the import of general goods, anthracite, culm and limestone. The limekiln still survives on the attractive harbour. Abercastle can claim a small piece of important maritime history; in 1876 the first man to sail solo across the Atlantic landed here. Half a mile west of the village, standing just off the coast path, is Carreg Samson, an excellent example of a Bronze Age burial chamber. The capstone is 15ft long and 9ft wide, and according to legend Samson placed it in position using only his little finger.

GOODWICK

Until the harbour was completed in 1906, Goodwick was nothing more than a cluster of fisherman cottages. As the new terminus for the main railway line from London, this one time village quickly adopted the status of a major ferry port and today is still the link between Fishguard and Rosslare in Ireland. Inevitably Goodwick has grown so close, in every sense, to its very near neighbour Fishguard that it is now virtually a suburb of the larger town and the two are synonymous.

FISHGUARD

DISTANCES: Haverforwest 16m, Milford Haven 22m, Narberth 24m, Pembroke 26m, Tenby 35m, Carmarthen 46m and London 272m

Fishguard and Goodwick, 16 miles northeast of St. Davids are the only parts of Pembrokeshire's outer coastline which are not within the National Park. The harbour is in fact the main sailing centre of the North Pembrokeshire coast. Before the harbour, Fishguard had established itself as a very busy port, with slate, corn, butter and cured pilchards and herrings representing the main exports. During the 18th century only Haverfordwest was handling a greater volume of trade. Shipbuilding was important too; the shipyard was renowned for its schooners and square-rigged vessels. The harbour and impressive breakwaters on the Goodwick side of the bay were built in 1906 to attract the transatlantic liners away from Liverpool and Southampton. But as was the reality for Milford Haven, Cardigan, New Quay and other hopeful West Wales ports, the big dream did not materialise. However, there was compensation in successfully establishing the ferry links with Ireland - a lasting and positive return on the massive task of constructing the breakwater, which consumed 800 tones of rock along every foot of its half a mile length. Fishguard has remained a major British ferry port with excellent port facilities. However, its biggest contribution to the history books occurred on 22nd February 1797, when the town was the scene of an extraordinary invasion which has the distinction of being the last invasion on British soil. The uninvited guests were members of a French expeditionary force under the command of an American-Irish adventurer, Colonel William Tate, who had a commission in the French army. His mission was to seize Bristol, at the time Britain's second city, but bad weather forced the ships to land at Carreg Wastad Point, northwest of Fishguard. Once ashore, Tate's troops set about pilfering farms and homesteads, gorging themselves with as much food as they could lay their hands on, washed down with barrels of spirits which local people

The Marine walk, Fishguard

Fishguard

Lower Town Fishguard

had salvaged from a recent shipwreck. In this somewhat unfit condition the soldiers approached the town and, according to local tradition, mistook a crowd of women in red shawls and tall hats for guardsmen. The leader of these women, Jemima Nicholas, a local cobblerwoman, is said to have captured a dozen Frenchmen single handed, armed with only a pitchfork. Her heroism is remembered in the form of a monument in the churchyard at St. Mary's, where she is buried. Within 48hrs of landing the French had surrendered. The heroism of the women has been painstakingly recorded in a vivid and carefully researched tapestry measuring 30 metres which superbly characterises the event. The tapestry is on permanent display in the Town Hall. Fishguard is split into two distinct parts. The busy upper part is much like any small town, with many shops, pubs and places to eat. The Lower Town is much older and very attractive, its pretty cottage clustered around the old harbour, where the River Gwaun reaches the sea. In 1971 Lower Fishguard temporarily changed its identity to the fictional town of Llareggub when this picturesque location was chosen for the the film version of Dylan Thomas's famous radio play "Under Milk Wood", and was also the location for the making of the Orson Welles classic "Moby Dick". The landscape around Fishguard is truly magnificent. To the northwest is the dramatic Stumble Head, where the lighthouse is linked to the cliff by a causeway. Dinas Head dominates the coast to the northeast, while inland is the beautiful wooded Gwaun Valley. The whole area is dotted with prehistoric sites.

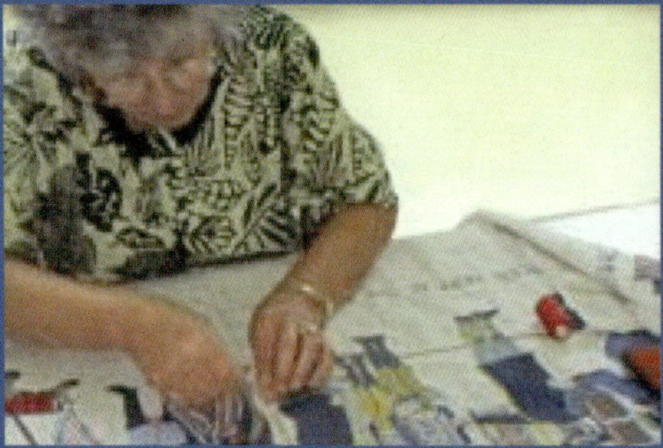

The Last Invasion Tapestry commemorates the last invasion of Britain, which took place near Fishguard on February 22nd 1797.

Around 1,400 French soldiers led by an American Colonel William Tate landed at Carreg Wastad on Strumble Head in an attempt to divert British troops away from Ireland, where the French planned a major attack.

The invading force pillaged farms and fought several skirmishes with local people in one of which Jemima Nicholas, a Fishguard cobbler, is reputed to have captured 12 soldiers single-handedly.

The embroidered 100ft long tapestry marking the event was initiated by Fishguard Arts Society as its contribution to the 1997 Bicentenary of the Last Invasion.

Designed by the late Elizabeth Cramp, the tapestry was worked on by more than 70 local stitchers, who spent over 40,000 hours working the finely detailed stitching in 178 different colours of wool.

Now internationally recognised as a major work of art, its format is based on the famous Bayeux Tapestry which tells the story of the 1066 Norman Invasion.

The specially designed Gallery showcasing the Last Invasion Tapestry is open during Library Hours Monday - Saturday

Admission is free.

Fishguard Last Invasion Tapestry Gallery

01437 776638

Opening Hours

April - September

Mon - Weds, Fri, Sat 9.30am - 5.00pm
Thursday 9.30am - 6.30pm

October - March

Mon - Weds, Fri 9.30 - 5.00pm
Thursday 9.30 - 6.30pm
Saturday 9.30am - 1.00pm

www.pembrokeshire.gov.uk/libraries

THE GWAUN VALLEY

The Gwuan Valley is exceptionally beautiful and runs inland from Lower Fishguard to its source high on the slopes of Foel Eryr in the Preseli Hills. It is one of several inland areas of Pembrokeshire which fall within the National Park, and is regarded by geologists as the best example in the British Isles, if not the world, of a sub-glacial meltwater channel. What this means is that about 200,000 years ago, towards the end of one of several recurring Ice Ages which have gripped the planet, the climate became progressively warmer and water began to tunnel beneath the melting ice. This meltwater was under intense pressure, the ice acting as a sort of geological pipe and moved with such tremendous force that it flowed uphill for long stretches. As this unstoppable water eventually crashed into the sea, taking with it huge bolders and blocks of ice, it created deep, sleep sided gorges in the landscape. Such are the awesome forces of nature which have given us the spectacular Gwaun Valley. The valley is narrow and sheltered, with heavily wooded sides stretching up to 200ft high. It is rich in wildlife and prehistoric remains, with an abundance of wild flowers and such birds as the buzzard, kestrel, owl, kingfisher, warbler and dipper. The river Gwaun, low and gentle in the summer, becomes a roaring torrent in winter as it rushes down from the Preseli Hills rising behind the valley. Most of the valley's small communities are centred around the hamlets of Llanychaer and Pontfaen. These are largely farming communities, as much of the valley floor is farmed and several farmhouses boast interesting architectural features such as distinctive Flemish style chimneys. The people of the valley are distinctive too, not in appearance, but in the fact that they are sticklers for local tradition. They still celebrate New Years Day on the 13th January according to the old Gregorian calendar - despite the fact that the change to the Julian calendar was made legal in 1752. Other interesting stones can be seen at the restored church in picturesque Pontfaen, where memorial stones dating from the 9th century stand in the churchyard. The ancient woodland of the Gwaun Valley is very precious, and parts of it have been designated as SSSI's (Sites of Special Scientific Interest). The species to be found here include oak, ash, sycamore, alder, blackthorn, hazel, hornbeam,

Newport

wild cherry and wych elm. The National Park Authority has established the Cilrhedyn Woodland Centre to promote good woodland management in the valley. Though very much a working centre for the Park Authority's woodland experts and rangers, it is planned to encourage visitors to the centre on a limited number of special open days during the main holiday season. More details of this can be obtained from any National Park Centre. The Golden Road Path takes you from Lower Fishguard to Crymych via the ridge of the Preseli Hills, passing such fascinating features as Bronze Age burial mounds, a Neolithic burial chamber, a particularly fine example of an Iron Age fort and Carn Meini - the source of the bluestone which thousands of years ago mysteriously found its way to Stonehenge for the construction of the monument's inner circle.

NEWPORT

The town of Newport is a very popular resort. The charming little town sits on the lower slopes of the Carn Ingli, which rises to more than 1100ft above sea level, and the superb stretch of sands on the east side of the Nevern estuary is rivalled only by Whitesands Bay as the best beach in North Pembrokeshire. On the opposite shore of the estuary mouth is Parrog. It was here that Newport developed as a thriving port engaged in fishing, coastal trading and shipbuilding. Newport was an important wool centre. However, this industry faltered when an outbreak of plague hit the town during the reign of Elizabeth I and much business was lost to Fishguard. Later in the port's development slates were quarried from local cliffs went by sea to Haverfordwest, Pembroke, Tenby and parts of Ireland. In 1825 maritime trade received a boost when the quay was built,

and come the end of the 19th century Newport boasted five warehouses, several limekilns, coal yards and a shipyard. Today the estuary is silted up and pleasure craft occupy the moorings. As far as the town itself, one of the main features is Newport Castle. This overlooks the estuary and was built in the early 13th century by William FitzMartin. It has had an eventful history: captured by Llywelyn the Great in 1215, then by Llywelyn the Last in 1257, and attacked and damaged in Owain Glyndwr's revolt in 1408, after which it fell into decline. It remained a ruin until 1859, when the gatehouse and one of its towers were converted into a residence. Today the castle is in private ownership and not open to visitors. You can, however, see William FitzMartin's other contribution to Newport. He established St. Mary's, a huge church which is cruciform in plan and features a 13th century Norman tower. Other attractions in Newport include a golf course alongside the sands and the prehistoric cromlech known as Carreg Goetan Arthur, which stands in a field by the bridge. There are many other such sites in the area. On Carn Ingli Common there are prehistoric hut circles and stones and the most famous and striking site of all is Pentre Ifan, 3 miles southeast of Newport.

PENRALLT GARDEN CENTRE

Set in 70 acres of farmland, woodland and coastal walks, the 3-acre nursery site has a vast area of glasshouses and tunnels - providing the ideal conditions for the enormous range of home-grown plants.

As a long-established business, which has grown over 25 years from one polytunnel, the Fletcher family and staff offer friendly, helpful advice on all aspects of gardening, along with high quality products to suit every garden situation and pocket.

Browse through what is probably the largest, most comprehensive - if you don't find what you're looking for, we'll do our very best to obtain it for you.

80% of plants are grown in our own Nursery and our policy is to source as much British grown stock as possible.

Situated right on the rugged North Pembrokeshire coastline, between Cardigan and Newport, the possibilities for coastal or woodland walks are endless, with stunning views in every direction.

After a walk or browse through our extensive produce, why not relax over a fresh coffee, tea or a home cooked meal in our Pavilion Café.

DINAS CROSS

Dinas Cross and its surrounding area is notable for its prehistoric monuments, especially the Bronze Age cairns. Cairns and barrows - mounds of earth or stone and earth - were built throughout the Bronze Age (2000 - 600BC) and often mark the sites of burials. Stone cists at the centre of the mound often contain cremations and pottery vessels and it is thought that the cairns themselves acted as burial sites. The stones for the first stone phase of Stonehenge came from Carn Meini, high in the Preselis. The whole area is littered with prehistoric sites including Iron Age hillforts (600BC - 43AD) and earlier cairns and standing stones. Sites like the spectacular hillfort at the summit of Carningli were clearly used over a long period of time and must have been important spiritual or religious places. Mynydd Melyn, a short distance southeast of Dinas Mountain, contains abundant evidence of prehistoric activity including hut circles (the foundations of pre-historic dwellings) parts of a field system and several cairns.

THE TEIFI ESTUARY

The River Teifi is a natural boundary that lies between Pembrokeshire and Ceredigion and its wide estuary is of great interest. The large and popular beach of Poppit Sands is backed by extensive dunes and has good visitor facilities. The area is also excellent walking and watersports country, and the estuary is a favourite haunt for birdwatchers. The many species to be observed here include gulls, oystercatchers curlews, cormorants and shelduck. The Teifi is also well known for its salmon and sea trout and the ancient Teifi coracle was used by fishermen long before the Romans arrived. The valley of the Teifi, which is a little further inland separates the counties of Ceredigion and Carmarthenshire, is said to be one of the most beautiful river valleys in Britain. It is certainly very scenic, with several picturesque towns and villages along its banks and for visitors to North Pembrokeshire is well worth exploring.

CILGERRAN

Famous for its superb Norman castle, which is perched above the wooded gorge of the Teifi, Cilgerran is a few miles east of Cardigan and was once a slate quarrymens village. It is the venue for the annual coracle regatta, which takes place in August.

Poppit Sands

Teifi Estuary

Nevern

St. Dogmaels

NEVERN

Nevern is an ancient parish on the River Nyfer, close to Newport. Its imposing Norman church, dedicated to the Celtic saint Brynach, has a definite mystique and atmosphere that is compounded by the famous bleeding yew in the churchyard, a broken branch that constantly drips blood red sap. The church features a magnificent 11th century wheel, headed Celtic cross. Above the church, topping a deep ravine, is Nevern Castle, a motte and baily earthwork.

MOYLEGROVE

This attractive coastal village stands on the Newport to St Dogmael's road, a mile from Ceibwr Bay. It dates back to Norman times and nearby are two burial chambers.

ST. DOGMAELS

Facing Cardigan across the Teifi estuary is the picturesque hillside of the village St Dogmaels. It lies close to Poppit Sands, the most northerly beach in the National Park and also at the northern end of the Pembrokeshire Coastal Path. In St Dogmaels you will find the remains of a 12th century abbey built in 1115 by Benedictine monks from France - as a replacement for an earlier Celtic monastery which had stood on the site until Viking raiders destroyed it in the 10th century. The north and west walls of the nave are still standing.

Nevern Churchyard

The Bleeding Yew

Kneelers made by the Ladies of the Church, Nevern

EVENTS & DAYS OUT GUIDE

JANUARY

New Year's Day swim. Saundersfoot
www.visit-saundersfoot.com

FEBRUARY

Melodies at the Manor
12th February
Scolton Manor

Narberth A Cappela festival
18th – 21st February Locations in Narberth

MARCH

Saundersfoot Cawl Factor 12th March
Regency Hall S/Foot

APRIL

Tenby BSRA Scooter Rally
29th – 2nd May
Tenby

Narberth Big Plant Sale
30th April
Town Moor

MAY

Tenby CARTEN
Bike Ride
7th May

Fishguard Folk Festival
27th – 30th

Really Wild Food & Countryside Festival
28th – 29th May St Davids

St Davids Cathedral Festival
27th – 5th June St Davids

Welsh Dragonboat Champs 29th May
Llys y Fran Country Park

Pembrokeshire Walking Festival
17th May – 1st June

JUNE

Pembrokeshire Fish Week
21st July – 6th August
Various Locations

JULY

Proms in the Castle
5th July
Pembroke Castle

Tenby Long Course
Week-End 8th – 10th July
Tenby

Fishguard International
Music Festival
July 19th – 30th July

Tenby 10K▯ 31st July Tenby

AUGUST

Tenby Fireman's Carnival
3rd August
Tenby

Pembroke/Lamphey Show
3rd August
Lamphey

Pembrokeshire County Show 16th,
17th, 18th Aug Haverfordwest

Abber Jazz Festival 25th – 29th
Fishguard

Cardigan River & Food Festival
6th August

Tenby Spectacular 3pm-10pm
Sunday 7th August
Sunday 14th August
Sunday 21th August
Sunday 28rd August

SEPTEMBER

Pembroke County Run
1st Sept
Motor Bikes & Vintage Cars

Milford Haven Music Festival
6th - 13th Sept

Red Bull Cliff Diving 10 – 11th Sept
Abereiddy

Ironman Wales 18th Sept Tenby

Iron Kids 17th Sept Tenby

Tenby Arts Festival
Sept 24th – 1st Oct
Tenby

Narberth Food Festival
Sept 24th – 25th
Queens Hall Narberth

OCTOBER

West Wales Wool Show
11th October
Queen's Hall Narberth

Saundersfoot Big Bang
Weekend 28th -29th
October Fireworks

NOVEMBER

Tenby Beer Festival 4th – 5th Nov Tenby

Blues Festival 11th – 13th Nov Tenby

DECEMBER

Saundersfoot Christmas Market
First Weekend Dec

Tenby Boxing Day Swim 11am□26th December

DAYS OUT GUIDE

Code Key

PARKING — CATERING FACILITIES — PICNIC AREA — UNDERCOVER/ WET WEATHER SUITABLE — FAMILY FRIENDLY — 10 MAP REF FOUND ON PAGE 3

(all information included within this section is provided by the restaurants in question and as such Eden Publications bear no responsibility as to accuracy)

35 MAP PG 3 — MANOR HOUSE WILDLIFE PARK

Experience close-up meetings with endangered animals from all over the world. Set in 52 acres of protected Pembrokeshire parkland, this is also a paradise for native flora and fauna. As seen on TV, our Wild Welsh Zoo has something for everyone – from close encounters with endangered animals from all over the world, to chilling out while the kids go wild on the front lawn, it's a place for all the family to enjoy.

Manor House, St Florence, Tenby SA70 8RJ
01646 651201 www.annaswelshzoo.co.uk

29 MAP PG 3 — BATTLEFIELD LIVE

BATTLEFIELD LIVE PEMBROKESHIRE

You may have tried Paintball or Airsoft, but aren't those sweaty masks irritating?. With Battlefield Live, because there are no physical projectiles, your shots are not affected by the wind, you do not have to wear masks, you do not get hurt and you are not weighed down with heavy padding. Infra-red reaches distances Paintballers can only dream of ... AND at night!!

Amroth Road, Llanteg, SA67 8QJ - 07777 671301,
www.battlefieldlivepembrokeshire.co.uk

6 MAP PG 3 — PEMBROKE CASTLE

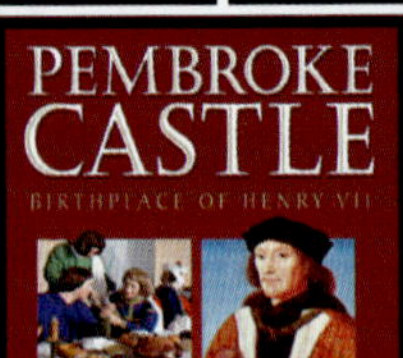

Idyllically set on the banks of the river estuary, this mighty fortress is largely intact, and its endless passages, tunnels and stairways are great fun to explore, plus there are super exhibitions, which tell the tale of its medieval life. Spend a day, and picnic in the beautifully kept grounds or from St. Anne's Bastion, enjoy views along the estuary while partaking of refreshments from the snack bar.

Pembroke, Pembrokeshire SA71 4LA
01646 684585, www.pembroke-castle.co.uk

40 MAP PG 3 CAREW CASTLE

The magnificent Carew Castle has a history spanning 2,000 years. Set in a stunning location, overlooking a 23-acre millpond, the castle displays the development from a Norman fortification to an Elizabethan country house. The site incorporates an impressive 11th century Celtic cross, the only restored tidal mill in Wales, a medieval bridge and a picnic area, all linked by a delightful one-mile circular walk which enjoys uninterrupted views of the castle and an easy access path suitable for wheelchairs and buggies.

Carew, Tenby, Pembrokeshire, SA70 8SL
01646 651782, www.pembrokeshirecoast.org.uk

4 MAP PG 3 MANORBIER CASTLE

With such a splendid setting overlooking a beautiful unspoilt beach, families love to explore Manorbier Castle and bring a little bit of history to life. The impressive Great Hall, Chapel and Turrets are dotted with life size figures - see children of the Tudor period and some prisoners in the dungeon. Enjoy delicious light bites and refreshments in the stylish cafe. Locally made cakes and icecreams, freshly ground coffee, and soup.

Manorbier, Tenby SA70 7SY
01646 621500, www.manorbiercastle.co.uk

34 MAP PG 3 CALDEY ISLAND

The Cistercian monks of Caldey continue a tradition which began there in Celtic times. More than a thousand years of prayer and quiet living have made this remote and beautiful island a haven of tranquillity and peace. The monks and islanders of Caldey are pleased to welcome day-visitors to share the delights of their island home throughout the summer season.

Caldey Island, off Tenby, SA70 7UJ
01834 844453, www.caldey-island.co.uk

31 MAP PG 3 OAKWOOD THEME PARK

Set in 80 acres of spectacular Pembrokeshire countryside, Oakwood is one of the UK's leading theme parks with more than 30 exhilarating attractions; including four world class rides to enjoy. Oakwood's unique combination of attractions also includes spectacular family rides, children's themed play areas and so much more.

Canaston Bridge, Narberth, Pembs, SA67 8DE
01834 891373, www.oakwoodthemepark.co.uk

1 MAP PG 207 — TALYLLYN RAILWAY

The Talyllyn Railway is a historic narrow-gauge steam railway, set in the beautiful Mid-Wales countryside. Running from Tywyn to Abergynolwyn and Nant Gwernol, the line passes the delightful Dolgoch Falls and there are excellent forest walks at Nant Gwernol.

Come and visit us for a great family day out.

Wharf Station, Tywyn, Gwynedd, LL36 9EY
01654 710472, www.talyllyn.co.uk/14

1 MAP PG 217 — ST CATHERINE'S WALK

Proudly claiming the title of Wales 'oldest town, Carmarthen has been able to mix new development with old traditions to make it an allweather visitor attraction. It has a range of leisure facilities, sporting activities and local attractions. Central to St Catherine 's Walk Shopping and entertainment Centre is Europe 's first all digital 3D multiplex Apollo Cinema which has all the latest movies.

St Catherine Street, Carmarthen SA31 1GA
01267 243040, www.stcatherineswalk.com

23 MAP PG 3 — LLYS-Y-FRAN COUNTRY PARK

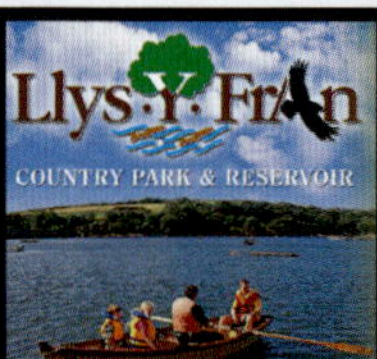

A visit to Llys-y-Fran Country Park and Reservoir has long been one of Pembrokeshire's favourite days out. There's such a wide variety to interest the whole family - from a short stroll to a full stretch walk, from cycling to rowing, or simply enjoying the spectacular views of the 100ft high dam and the surrounding countryside... the list is endless and we're sure you'll want to come back again and again.

Clarbeston Road, Haverfordwest, SA63 4RR
01437 532273, john.sampson@dwrcymru.com

36 MAP PG 3 — PICTON CASTLE

There's plenty to do at Picton Castle every day! Our 40 acres of woodlands are a treasure trove of wild plants thriving alongside showy exotics to delight gardeners.There's nearly 2 miles of paths, with strategically placed benches so you can take a brisk walk or a leisurely stroll and enjoy the birdsong and views.

Haverfordwest, Pembrokeshire, SA62 4AS
Tel: 01437 751326, www.pictoncastle.co.uk

56 MAP PG 3 CLERKENHILL ADVENTURE FARM

Clerkenhill Adventure Farm and Frizbee Golf Course

Come along and take a stroll around our Adventure Trail. The unspoiled natural woodland is the perfect backdrop to this family fun trail. Our 18 basket Frizbee Golf course is spread over 10 acres of a valley adjoining Clerkenhill Adventure Farm. You are surrounded by beautiful countryside with trees and streams surrounding the course.

Slebech, Haverfordwest, SA62 4PE
Tel: 01437 751227 www.clerkenhill.co.uk

32 MAP PG 3 FOLLY FARM

Folly Farm

With six fun-filled amusement and activity zones, some of which are undercover, there is something for everyone to enjoy. So, when you are looking for fun things to do for all the family, whatever the weather, look no further than Folly Farm. Come and see our Jolly Farm animals or ride on the fairground rides in our indoor Funfair. Enjoy our outdoor Adventure Parks and Carousel Woods indoor Adventure Playground. Visit Follywood Country Park and our very own Zoo.

Begelly, Kilgetty, Pembrokeshire, SA68 0XA
Tel: 01834 812731 www.folly-farm.co.uk

47 MAP PG 3 HILTON COURT GARDENS & CRAFT CENTRE

Gardens & Craft Centre HILTON COURT

Hilton Court, one of Pembrokeshire's best keep secrets. Situated in 12 acres of outstanding beauty, in the National Coastal Park to the west of Haverfordwest in Pembrokeshire, West Wales. Visitors are drawn to the beauty and tranquility of the delightful gardens and the breath-taking location overlooking St Brides Bay. At the centre you will find a Gallery, Pottery, Shops, Gardens, Tea Room and a Restaurant.

Roch, Haverfordwest,
Pembrokeshire , SA62 6AE
Garden Centre Tel: 01437 710262
Restaurant Tel: 01437 711000
www.hiltongardensandcrafts.co.uk

1 MAP PG 207 VALE OF RHEIDOL RAILWAY

Vale of Rheidol Light Railway Company Incorporated 1897

A blast of the whistle and the hiss of steam and you're away! Sit back, relax and let us take you on a nostalgic journey through some of Wales' most spectacular scenery. Travelling on the Vale of Rheidol Railway is the finest way to see the stunning Rheidol Valley. Opened in 1902, the railway has been delighting passengers young and old for over a century.

Park Avenue, Aberystwyth, Ceredigion, SY23 1PG
Tel: 01970 625819, www.rheidolrailway.co.uk

INLAND PEMBROKESHIRE

In the ancient Welsh tales of The Mabinogion, Pembrokeshire was described as "Gwlad hud a lledrith" - the land of magic and enchantment. Nowhere is this more evident than in the wild , mysterious Preseli Hills. These rolling moorlands, often overlooked by visitors on their way to the coast, are the major upland region of the National Park, presenting a stark contrast to the relatively flat coastal plateau. The evidence left by the earliest settlers suggests man has occupied the hills for at least 5000 years. Neolithic burial chambers, Bronze Age cairns, stone circles, standing stones and Iron Age forts litter this untouched Celtic landscape.

An alternative way of exploring the Preseli Hills is to join a guided walk or horse riding lesson which are run by the National Park Authority, as part of its annual activities and events programme. For more information contact any National Park Information Centre.

LLYS-Y-FRAN RESERVOIR & COUNTRY PARK

Close to the picturesque village of Rosebush, beautiful Llys-y-Fran Country Park incorporates the 212 acre reservoir that supplies most of Pembrokeshire's drinking water. Around this man made lake are mature woodlands and open grassland, with superb views of the Preseli Hills and surrounding farmland. In spring the carpets of bluebells in the woods are a sheer delight and throughout the season the country park is vibrant with the colours of countless varieties of wild flowers. In recent years improvements have been made to the park, following a scheme to increase the size of the reservoir. An example of which is the much wider footpath right round the reservoir and the 20, 000 broad leafed trees which have been planted. As a result the six and a half mile perimeter walk is now even more enjoyable than ever.

Mountain bikes are another treat that families can enjoy. Bikes can be hired by the hour, and with the reservoir perimeter path serving as a cycle track, this can be a fun activity in which everyone can participate. Fishing is another leisure pursuit which has always been popular here, and Llys-y-Fran attracts anglers from all over Wales and beyond. Little wonder as few fisheries can match the country park's excellent facilities. These include a purpose built boathouse with a fleet of loch-style petrol engine fishing boats ideal for fly fishermen. During the season over 20,000 top quality rainbow trout are released into the freedom of the lake from their rearing cages. A healthy population of brown trout adds variety to the sport. For watersport enthusiasts the reservoir is perfect both for beginners and for more experienced sailors. The park shop does however offer launching permits for dinghies, sailboards and canoes. As you would expect in a country park of Llys-y-Fran's status and reputation, wildlife is of prime concern in the management of the park. The oak and coniferous woodlands and rough grass provide ideal habitats for a variety of birds. More than 140 species have been recorded here. Llys-y-Fran licensed cafe enjoys superb views across the reservoir and countryside and is housed in the Visitor Centre alongside the gift and souvenir shop. The cafe offers excellent service, home-made food and Sunday roasts, it is open from the 1st of March. It is also worth noting that Llys-y-Fran Country Park has strong historical and musical connections. Near the base of the reservoir dam is a tumble down cottage, the birth place of the famous Welsh composer William "Penfro" Rowlands. It was in gratitude for his son's recovery from a serious illness that he was inspired to write the tune for Blaenwern, one of the best loved of all hymn tunes. A monument to William Rowlands, erected by Welsh Water now stands near the ruins of the old cottage.

for further information
tel: 01437 532273
or 01437 532694

ROSEBUSH

Rosebush enjoys an unusual if modest claim to fame, slates from its quarries were used to roof the Houses of Parliament. But the village could have become a well known tourist attraction in the 19th century had everything gone according to plan. When the Clunderwen - Maenclochog railway opened in 1876 to serve the quarry there were big ambi-[illegible] develop Rosebush as an

inland spa. A small tourist industry did develop here, but nothing like on the scale imagined.Rosebush is close to Llys-y-Fran Reservoir and Country Park and stands below the summit of Foel Cwm Cerwyn, in a superb setting which is ideal for walking. In 1992 a visitor centre and museum was opened in the village's old post office.

MYNACHLOGDDU

This small pastoral community of the Preseli Hills once belonged to the monastery at St. Dogmaels. It stands east of Rosebush, close to the impressive Gors Fawr Stone Circle, which is over 70ft in diameter. A commemorative stone to the poet Waldo Williams is also nearby.

NEW MOAT

This small village stands in the Preseli foothills, just east of Llys-y-Fran Country Park. A mound marks the site of a Norman motte and bailey castle. The church, distinctive for its tall tower, has an early 17th century altar tomb.

MAENCLOCHOG

A small Victorian church on the village green is the central feature of this sprawling community on the southern slopes of the Preseli Hills, a couple of miles north east of Llys-y-Fran Country Park. For many years the village has served the needs of the area and early this century Maenclochog boasted a blacksmith, miller, carpenter, lime burner, wheelwright, draper and no fewer than 10 pubs. A mile from the village is Penrhos, the only thatched cottage in the area and is now a museum.

CRYMYCH

Crymych, situated on the A478 Tenby to Cardigan road, is a 19th century hillside village which grew up around the railway. The Whitland Cardigan line was completed in 1880 and no longer exists, but the village has remained an important agricultural centre and an ideal base from which to

explore the Preseli Hills. Within easy reach are Foel Drygarn, where cairns and an early Iron Age fort are to be found and the 1300ft summit of Y Frenni Fawr.

BONCATH

Between Crymych and Newcastle Emlyn, Boncath takes its name from the Welsh word for buzzard. A former railway village, it is notable for two houses - Ffynone, designed by John Nash in 1792 and Cilwendeg, a Georgian house built by Morgan Jones.

EGLWYSWRW

A compact little village near Castell Henllys Iron Age fort, north of the Preseli Hills, this place with the unpronounceable name, is where St. Wrw is buried. The pre-Christian churchyard is circular and other interesting historical features include the medieval inn, the remains of a motte and bailey castle and a prehistoric ringwork.

CASTELL HENLLYS IRON AGE FORT

This remarkable and archaeological important example of an Iron Age fort is managed by the National Park Authority and has been partially reconstructed with thatched roundhouses, animal pens, a smithy and a grain store. Recently the site was the location of the BBC's "Surviving the Iron Age" series. The Visitor Centre houses an exhibition which serves as an introduction to the life of the early Celts in Wales. Castell Henllys probably flourished between the 4th century BC and the 1st century AD, when the Romans began their conquest of Britain. The Iron Age Celts were a fierce and warlike people and many of their chieftains lived in well defended forts, of which Castell Henllys was typical. Sited on a valley spur, it had natural defences on three sides, and where the spur joined the side of the valley massive earthworks were thrown up, topped with timber palisades. Stone walling protected a narrow gateway which can still be seen. Such elaborate defences would have employed a huge labour force and this suggests that Castell Henllys was occupied by a leader of some importance along with family, retainers and even a band of warriors. The introduction to the site of domestic animals which flourished in the Iron Age has given a further insight into the daily life of these ancient ancestors. A self guided trail takes you through Castell Henllys with information interpretive panels along the way. This is a wonderful place for schools and study groups and an Education Centre has been built in the valley below

Castell Henllys

Castell Henllys

Castell Henllys

the fort. To further recapture the atmosphere and spirit of this mystical historic site, which stands in beautiful North Pembrokeshire countryside below the summit Carn Ingli, special events are held throughout the holiday season, including shows given by the Prytani, an Iron Age Celtic reenactment group. Castell Henllys, just off the A486 a few miles east of Newport, is open daily from Easter to October.

tel: 01239 891319
www.castellhenllys.com

THE LANDSKER BORDERLANDS

When the Normans invaded Pembroke in 1093 and took the site on which the magnificent castle now stands, they were quick to consolidate their domination of South Pembrokeshire and the lands they had gained here. To the north of the county the rebellious Welsh proved more troublesome. The Norman response was to build a line of castles to protect their newly won territory, effectivcly dividing north from south.These formidable fortresses stretched from Llanstephan in the southeast to Roch in the northwest. They marked what has become known as the Landsker Line, a word of Norse origin meaning frontier. Originally a military device, the Landsker evolved into a cultural and linguistic divide and its effects are evident even today. For example, in the north of the county Welsh is still spoken and many of the place nanes are Welsh also. Churches are usually small, with bellcotes and no towers. By comparison in the anglicised south, English is the dominant language as is clear from the names of the towns and villages, and the Norman churches are characterised by tall, square towers which served as lookouts. One of the castles of the Landsker Line was Narberth. Its scant ruins still stand near the centre of this important market town, which is 10 miles north of Tenby. Narberth is at the heart of a beautiful and historic part of Inland Pembrokeshire known as the Landsker Borderlands. The Borderlands spill over into old Carmarthenshire and are bounded by the River Taf to the east, the Daugleddau estuary to the west, hills and valleys to the north and vales and plains to the south. As awareness of the Borderlands increases a growing number of visitors are exploring this largely undiscovered area of great rural delights. The attractive countryside of the Landsker Borderlands, rich in heritage and wildlife, is typified in the north by lush farmland sweeping down from the Preseli Hills.

Narberth Castle

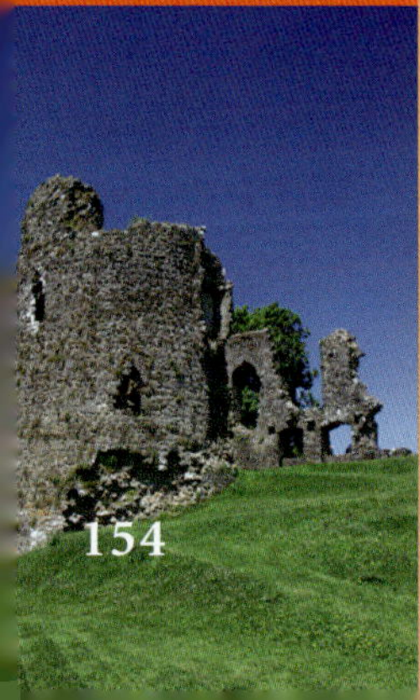

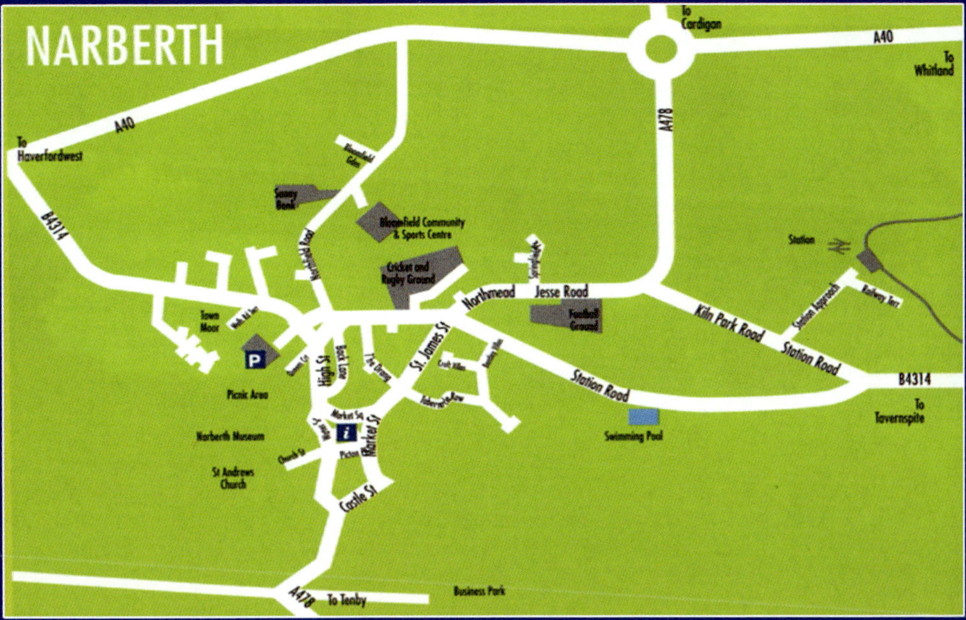

NARBERTH

DISTANCES: Fishguard 24m, Haverfordwest 9m, Milford Haven 14m, Pembroke 15m, St. Davids 25m, Tenby 10m, Carmarthen 21m and London 241m

This delightful little town, with its colour-washed Georgian houses, castle ruins and amazing variety of original shops is an essential visit. In recent years the town has become a centre for artists and craftspeople, many of whose works are sold here. Jewellery, pottery, paintings, fabrics, glassware, clothing and woodworks are all represented. Some of the shops and galleries sell a variety of goods while others specialise in the makers' own work.

Narberth

Narberth

Narberth Castle

Narberth

Narberth Town Hall

This creative movement may be relatively recent but Narberth's history is a long and fascinating one. Standing just south of the Landsker, it falls into the area regarded as "Little England beyond Wales" but its roots lie deep in Welsh history, culture and tradition. The Welsh princes of Dyfed lived here in the dark ages and the town, called by its Welsh name Arberth, features in the ancient stories of the Mabinogion. Narberth castle of which little now remains, was part of the Norman frontier separating north from south. It was captured by the Welsh on numerous occasions and destroyed by Cromwell's forces during the Civil War. Narberth is also remembered for the infamous Rebecca Riots of the 19th century. These began in 1839 with the burning of toll gates in Efailwen, a hamlet in the Preseli foothills a few miles north of the town. This anger was in response to the decision by rich landowners to impose crippling road tolls on the small and impoverished farming communities. The men responsible for torching the toll gates avoided recognition by dressing in women's clothing and blackening their faces, and they addressed their leader as "Rebecca". The dispute quickly became more widespread and other toll gates were destroyed just as quickly as they could be erected. The riots often described as a "true people's revolt" because they had their cause in natural justice, went on for a period of several years. It is one of the ironies of local history that when the authorities called out the troops in a bid to discover the identity of Rebecca and his followers, they were billeted in Narberth's poor house. Rebecca's Cell can be seen under the old Town Hall which now houses a craft shop. Narberth Castle of which little now remains, was part of the Norman frontier separating north from south. It was captured by the Welsh on numerous occasions and destroyed in the Civil War by Cromwell's forces. The castle ruins have been consolidated and are now open to the public all year. Narberth's small but attractive town centre is distinctive for its Town Hall and pleasant Georgian houses. With the promotion of the Landsker Borderlands and other rural areas, Narberth has been revitalised. PLANED (Pembrokeshire Local Action Network for Enterprise and Development) has its headquarters here and the town is very close to a number of the county's most popular attractions such as, Heron's Brook Golf Course, Oakwood, Canaston Bowl, Picton Castle, Llawhaden Castle, Holgan Camp Iron Age Hillfort and Folly Farm. These are in addition to those places of interest in Narberth itself, which include a wealth of interesting and unusual shops featuring antiques, art and crafts and galleries as well as many varied and interesting places to eat.

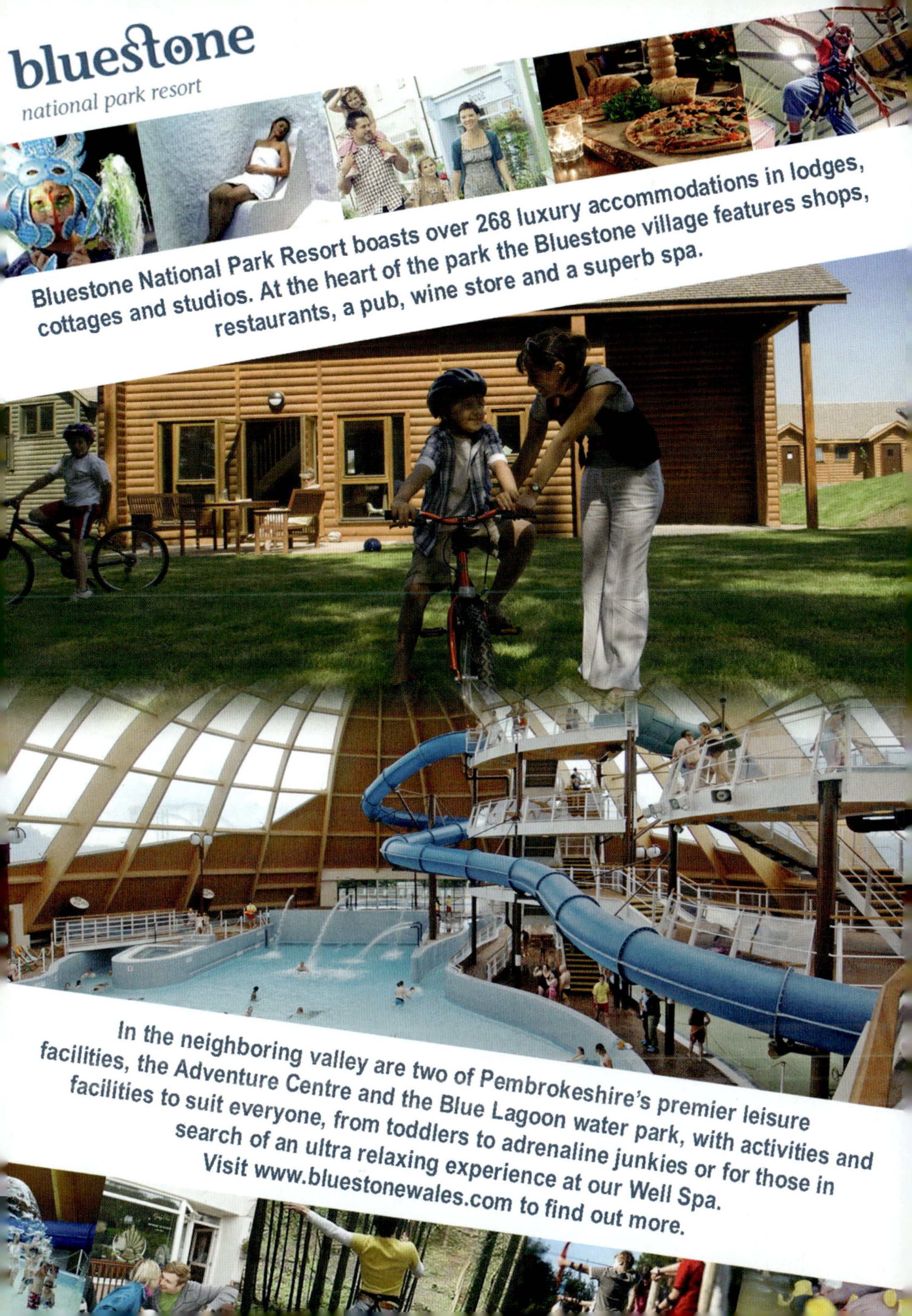
bluestone
national park resort
Bluestone National Park Resort boasts over 268 luxury accommodations in lodges, cottages and studios. At the heart of the park the Bluestone village features shops, restaurants, a pub, wine store and a superb spa.
In the neighboring valley are two of Pembrokeshire's premier leisure facilities, the Adventure Centre and the Blue Lagoon water park, with activities and facilities to suit everyone, from toddlers to adrenaline junkies or for those in search of an ultra relaxing experience at our Well Spa.
Visit www.bluestonewales.com to find out more.

NARBERTH SHOPPING

AUDREY BULL ANTIQUES
15 High Street
Tel: 01834 861199

THE MALTHOUSE
Back Lane
Tel: 01834 860303

CELTIC VISION
66 ST JAMES ST
NARBERTH. SA67 7DB
Tel: 01834 869123
www.celtic-vision.co.uk
Binoculars, cameras & camera equipment

ANDREW REES
29 High Street
Tel: 01834 861892

NO 47
47 High Street
Tel: 01834 869110

LIZ'S BAKERY
12 High Street
Tel: 01834 861039

NOBLES
4 High St
Tel: 01834 861135

POST OFFICE
9 High St
Tel: 01834 861337

THE CREATIVE CAFE
Spring Gardens
Tel: 01834 861651

THE WELSH FARMHOUSE COMPANY
35, High Street
Tel: 01834 861123

NEXT DOOR FLORIST
21 High Street
Tel: 01834 861032

FABRIC HOUSE
6 High Street
Tel: 01834 861063

WISEBUYS
18, High Street
Tel: 01834 861880

GOLDEN SHEAF
25 High Street
Tel: 01834 860407

HAULFRYN
13 High Street
Tel: 01834 861902

JELLY EGG
The Old Town Hall
Tel: 01834 860061

ANIMAL KITCHEN BOOKSHOP
Moorfield Terrace
Tel: 01834 860811

www.narberth.co.uk
www.narberthfoodfestival.co.uk
www.thequeenshall.org.uk
www.narberthmuseum.co.uk
www.thenarberthgallery.co.uk
www.pembrokeshire.gov.uk

CLUNDERWEN

Situated just inside Carmathenshire and known until the 1870's as Narbeth Road. The village of Clunderwen developed with the coming of the railway in 1852. An interesting historical anecdote is that it was here in 1913 that the James Brothers first flew their biplane - one of the earliest flights in Wales.

EFAILWEN

Efailwen is recorded in the history books as the place where the erection of a toll gate in 1839 sparked off the Rebecca Riots. Nearby at Glandy Cross is a group of Neolithic and Bronze Age sites, regarded as the most important in South Wales.

LAMPETER VELFREY

There are several prehistoric sites in the immediate area, including tumuli, a Bronze Age hearth and three Neolithic burial chambers.

LLANBOIDY

Llanboidy lies across the border in old Carmarthenshire, about 5 miles north of Whitland, in the small Gronw Valley. A well in the village was the focus of many medieval pilgrimages. Close to Llanboidy are two ancient sites, a cromlech at Cefn Brafle and Arthur's Table, a tumulus, which is in a wood at Dolwilym. Today the village enjoys fame as the home of Pemberton's Victorian Chocolates.

Llawhaden Castle

GELLI

Located just north of Llawhaden, the small community of Gelli developed around a large woollen mill. This worked from the late 19th century until 1937 and was one of several mills which flourished in the Landsker Borderlands at that time. Fishing was another important industry here. In the late 19th century 6 pairs of Cleddau coracles fished here between Gelli and Llawhaden.

LLAWHADEN

Llawhaden was an important medieval settlement standing on the Landsker Line. The original Norman castle was later developed as a magnificent bishops palace by the Bishop's of St. Davids. The ruins which stand today are evidence of the grandeur of this fortified palatial residence. You can also see the remains of a medieval hospice chapel. The Norman church of St. Aidan stands in the valley below, on the banks of the Eastern Cleddau, in a very picturesque position.

LLAWHADEN CASTLE

Originally a wooden structure built in Norman times, the castle was rebuilt by the Bishops of St. Davids between the late 13th and 15th centuries and transformed into a great fortified palace. This comprised several buildings set around a five sided courtyard, strengthened with angled corners. The ruins now in the care of CADW (Welsh Historic Monuments), include the front of the gatehouse which still stands to its full height, the Great Hall, bakehouse, barracks, visitors' lodgings and the Chapel of the Blessed Virgin. After using the castle for more than 250 years, the bishops dismantled it and stripped the lead from the roof. Close to the castle are two other historic attractions - a restored medieval hospice and Holgan Camp, an Iron Age fort to which visitors now have access thanks to the opening of a new public footpath. The site of the camp was overgrown for centuries until cleared and fenced by PLANED and CADW. Holgan Camp had formidable defences and is a well preserved example of an Iron Age defended enclosure. Many such camps were established in the area.

Llawhaden Castle Gatehouse

Llawhaden Castle

Ludchurch

LLANDDEWI VELFREY

Located between Narberth and Whitland on the busy A40, Llanddewi Velfrey originally grew around its ancient church and there is evidence of occupation during the Iron Age. The Quaker burial ground also reflects a strong tradition of non-conformity. The area around the village is ideal for country walks with stunning views of the Marlais Valley to the south and the Preseli Hills to the north.

LLANDISSILIO

This village stands on the A478 north of Narberth, a road which has developed from a prehistoric route that linked the Preseli Hills and the Cleddau estuary. Castle sites and earthworks suggest that the parish has a long history, an idea supported by the inscribed stones in the church which date back from the 5th or 6th century.

LLANGOLMAN

From Efailwen, on the A478, the road to Llangolman gives breathtaking views of the approaching Preseli Hills. Until a few years ago, this small village encompassed the last working Pembrokeshire slate quarry Gilfach. The slate, which was formed from volcanic ash, is a lovely soft green colour and was highly prized. The slate was used to roof the National Library of Wales in Aberystwyth and to line the Suez Canal. The Slate Workshop, on the outskirts of the village, still uses some of the green Pembrokeshire slate, although the majority now comes from other Welsh quarries.

ROBESTON WATHEN

The earliest record of Robeston Wathen dates back as far as 1282. The small hilltop community, on the A40, has a Norman Church and distinctive tower. The part of the parish name Robeston is of Norman origin, whose Kings sought to impose their rule on this part of Wales. The Parish was called at this time Villa Robti or "Robert's Ton" although no records indicate who Robert was. However in the 13th century a family by the name Wathen was granted the titular Lordship of the Manor, and so the village has been named Robeston Wathen ever since. This family had interests in the production and weaving of wool, which was to remain the major export of England and Wales for several centuries. Some indication of the importance of this trade can be seen from

Robeston Wathen

the fact that Geoffrey Chaucer, the author of Canterbury Tales, earned his living as the Kings Wool Talleyman. Today he would have been called a Chief Inspector of Customs and Excise. The Wathen family moved to the Cotswolds, Gloucester and Bristol in Elizabethan times - then great centres of the wool trade. The Wathen family have served with distinction in Church, State and banking. One John de Wathen became Bishop of Salisbury and his 14th century tomb can be seen in Westminster Abbey.

REYNALTON

Reynalton, situated west of Begelly and south of Narberth, is now a small, quiet hamlet in the midst of farmland. Yet earlier in the century coal mining was a thriving local industry, as the village stands in the old South Pembrokeshire coalfield.

TAVERNSPITE

Tavernspite is on the Pembs/Carms border at the junction of the B4328 and B4314. At one time this was also on the route of the mail coaches which travelled from London to Ireland via Milford Haven. The local community here takes great pride in the village; in recent years Tavernspite has won awards in competitions for Wales In Bloom and Best Kept Village. Tavernspite is also notable for its chapel, one of the most remote and picturesque in Pembrokeshire.

LUDCHURCH

Located less than 3 miles south-east of Narberth, Ludchurch stands on the route of the Knightway footpath. A curious fact is that prior to the 1950's the name Ludchurch referred only to the Norman church and parish and the village itself was known as Egypt. There are definitely no pyramids here, but there are some fine lime kilns to be seen in the old quarry. The name Ludchurch is also becoming increasingly known among people with good taste. The reason is Princes Gate Water - a spring water of exceptionally pure quality which has proved so popular that it is now supplied all over Wales and to markets as far apart as London and North America. The water comes from 3 acres of farmland in the parish which are saturated with clear natural springs.

Tavernspite

Templeton

Oakwood

CANASTON BRIDGE

Just west of Narberth Canaston Bridge marks the junctions of the A40 and A4075. This attractive wooded area is the northern boundary of the Eastern Cleddau and from here you can join the Knightsway - a 9 mile walk linking the Daugleddau Trail with the coast path at Amroth. Nearby, on the south side of the A40 is a picnic area and restored Blackpool Mill. A mile or so from the north side is the impressive ruins of Llawhaden Castle. A few miles south on the A4075 are the neighbouring attractions of Oakwood and CC2000. Also within the area are several interesting woodland walks, including a relatively short path which takes you to Blackpool Mill.

OAKWOOD

One of the top ten theme parks in the UK, Oakwood has over 40 rides and attractions for all the family.

BLUESTONE & THE BLUE LAGOON

Set within Pembrokeshire Coast National Park, Bluestone boasts luxury accommodation in lodges, cottages and studios. The Bluestone village features shops, restaurants, a pub, wine store and a superb spa, while in the neighbouring valley are two of Pembrokeshire's premier leisure facilities: the Adventure Centre and the Blue Lagoon water park.

Blue Lagoon

Bluestone

Beside the Daugleddau

TEMPLETON

The layout of Templeton which is a mile south of Narberth, is a fine example of village planning in the Middle Ages. It is believed that the Knights Templars had a hospice here, possibly on the site now occupied by St. John's church, and in the 13th century the village was known as the settlement of the Templars. Hence the name Templeton today. There are several ancient sites here, including Sentence Castle, originally a raised fortification which also probably dates from the time of the Knights Templars. The Knightsway Trail passes through the village.

WISTON

The village of Wiston, five miles northeast of Haverfordwest, was an important settlement in medieval times. Wiston Castle was at a strategic point on the Landsker Line and as such was the scene of much bloodshed in the 12th and 13th centuries. The remains of this impressive motte and bailey castle are a short walk from the car park in the centre of the village and now administered by CADW. Admission is free.

THE DAUGLEDDAU

The Daugleddau estuary is an area of great natural beauty, comprising the fascinating stretch of waterway which extends inland from the Haven and encompasses four rivers Western Cleddau, Eastern Cleddau, Carew and Cresswell. It is an inner sanctuary, often described as the hidden treasure of the Pembrokeshire Coast National Park. Daugleddau (which means two

The Daugleddau

rivers at the Cleddau) begins east of the Cleddau toll bridge, and has become known as The Secret Waterway. In recognition of the Daugleddau's remarkable diversity of flora and fauna, many parts of the waterway are designated Sites of Special Scientific Interest. These include the Carew and Cresswell rivers, Lawrenny Wood, Minwear Wood, parts of Slebech Park and West Williamston Quarries. In Tudor times Lawrenny was famous for its oysters. By the 19th century sailing vessels of all shapes and sizes, brigantines, ketches, sloops, schooners and coasters, were busily importing and exporting coal, grain, limestone, timber and general goods. Towards the latter part of the century, Willy Boys (flat barge like craft) - carried local produce and ran a shuttle service between seagoing vessels and the Daugleddau's upper reaches. The poor acidic soils of West Wales made lime a valuable and highly saleable commodity. Limestone was quarried at West Williamston, Garron Pill and Llangwm Ferry and burned in hundreds of kilns along thc waterway and coastline, from South Pembrokeshire to Cardigan Bay. The remains of several kilns are still visible. The band of carboniferous coal measures which runs across Pembrokeshire from St. Bride's Bay to Saundersfoot cuts through the uppermost reaches of the Daugleddau, and mining around Landshipping was at its height in the first half of the 19th century, particularly after the introduction in 1800 of the first steam engine to be used in a Pembrokeshire coalfield. The high quality anthracite was in great demand. A tragic accident at the Garden Pit near Landshipping in 1844 and a series of insurmountable geological problems which plagued the coalfield throughout its working life led to a rapid decline of the industry by the early 20th century. The last colliery to work, at Hook on the Western Cleddau, was closed by the National Coal Board in 1949. The waterway's rich oak woodlands helped encourage boatbuilding and cutters, smacks and schooners were built at yards and quays along the Daugleddau. At Lawrenny alone, over 40 sailing vessels were built during the first half of the 19th century.

Lawrenny

Burton

Pembroke Dock

Picton Castle

Tenby Harbour

Carew Mill

Other industries flourished too, from a chemical works at Whalecomb to a furnace and forge which operated on the site now occupied by Blackpool Mill. During the 19th century over 100 men earned their living by compass net fishing, a traditional method, suited to rivers with fast flowing tidal currents, which required considerable skill and courage. Much of the working life of the Daugleddau centred around Lawrenny Quay, which in its heyday had more than one quay. Today it is noted for its Yacht Station and excellent facilities for pleasure craft and seeing the waterway from the comfort of a boat will take you to places inaccessible by any other means. Whatever your method of exploration, the Daugleddau will provide endless relaxation and enjoyment. Sights worth seeking out are many and varied, including Lawrenny village and its well restored cottages and huge Norman church. A National Park picnic site gives superb views over the Carew and Cresswell rivers. At Cresswell Quay, a picnic site and pub are just yards from the water's edge where Kingfishers and herons feed in full view. The long distance Daugleddau Trail and other footpaths reveal a succession of delights, from the evocative ruins of magnificent Carew Castle to the ancient woodland of Minwear. There are many other historic sites to enjoy, such as the exotic gardens of Upton Castle and Picton Castle and the restored mills at Carew and Blackpool. The lime stone quarries have long since fallen silent, but today West Williamston is the centre of other important work for the waterway, the rescue, nursing and rehabilitation of injured and contaminated seabirds, at the Oiled Bird Rescue Centre. Regular visitors to the centre each year are substantial numbers of Manx shearwaters, which once blown inland by autumn gales are unable to take off again and are often stranded in brightly lit harbours and resorts such as Tenby.

Quayside Lawrenny Tearoom

Burton

BURTON

Sitting just across the Cleddau toll bridge from Pembroke Dock, and close to Neyland, Burton is a small hillside village which enjoys superb views over the waterway. It is best known as a boating centre and for its popular waterfront pub, which as well as good food boasts a large beer garden and panoramic views over the estuary to the south, east and west.

CAREW

The most southerly point of the Daugleddau section of the National Park, Carew is famous for its magnificent riverside castle, fine Celtic cross and restored tidal mill. There is also a picnic site and car park here, accessible from the village across the old narrow bridge. The village itself is small, neat and has a distinct charm, with a pub and a bridge. The village itself is small, neat and has a distinct charm, with a pub and a restaurant offering plenty of local hospitality. Close to Carew, on the south side of the A477, is the slumbering hamlet of Carew Cheriton. The church here dates from the late 14th century and is distinctive for its very tall tower, which has a corner steeple. In the churchyard there is a detached mortuary chapel.

Carew Castle

CAREW CASTLE

Here is a castle which has everything: magnificent ruins, an evocative setting, a long and important history, examples of medieval and Elizabethan architecture, a Celtic cross which is one of the finest in Wales and archaeological deposits dating back over the last 2000 years Carew is undoubtedly a king among castles. It stands on a low limestone ridge at the head of a tidal inlet of the Carew river - a strategic position, as it guarded a crossing of the river and the main road to Pembroke, 5 miles away. In times of war it could also be supplied by boat, as it has access to the open sea via the Daugleddau and the Haven waterway. Carew Castle was occupied continuously from the 12th century to the end of the 17th century, during which time it was gradually transformed from a medieval fortress to an Elizabethan mansion of consid erable splendour. Most photographs today tend to emphasise the latter, as the castle is often shot from across the water of Carew Pill to capture one of the ruin's most striking features - the great Renaissance north wing. which Sir John Perrot began building in 1588. Perrot died in 1592 of natural causes while imprisoned in the Tower of London and the wing was never completed. In April 1507 the castle and nearby Carew Meadows were the site of the Great Tournament - a spectacular 5 day event, attended by over 600 noblemen. The occasion was in honour of the Tudor monarchy and also to celebrate the fact that Henry VII had bestowed upon Sir Rhys ap Thomas, who held the castle at the time, the Order of the Knight of the Garter. Sir Rhys had played a major part in Henry's victory at Bosworth and was knighted on the battlefield; it is even said that Richard III died at his hands. Although the king himself was not in attendance, the tournament was a grand affair on a scale not previously seen in Wales. The huge assembly enjoyed jousting, sword displays, hunting and other sports of the day, and the Great Hall was the scene of a sumptuous banquet. This was the last event of its kind ever staged in Britain. During the Civil War years of 1644 and 1645, the castle changed hands between royalist and parliamentarian forces no fewer than four times. Towards the end of the century it was abandoned by the Carew family and fell into decline. The exciting thing about Carew Castle is that much is still being discovered about its very early history. Since 1986 it has been the subject of a phased but very intensive archaeological survey involving excavation, a stone by stone study of the surviving walls and buildings and examination of documents. To date, two major surprises have been unearthed. One is that the Norman part of the castle is much bigger and older than previously suspected. The other discovery of pre-Norman fortifications, adding weight to speculation that the site had a royal significance long before the Normans arrived and was the seat of Welsh kings throughout the Roman and Dark Age periods. This idea is supported by the famous Carew Cross, which stands within the Castle Field and is a memorial to a Welsh king who died in 1035, more than half a century before the Normans took Pembroke in 1093. In the near future, visitors to the castle will be able to see some of the discoveries made by the archaeological survey, as there are plans to build an Interpretation Centre on site. The castle is still privately owned by descendants of the Carew family, but is leased to the Pembrokeshire Coast National Park Authority under a 99 year agreement so that the castle and its surrounding earthworks can be conserved for everyone's enjoyment. Carew is the only castle managed by the National Park Authority.

for more information
tel: 01646 651782

CAREW CROSS

Carew's famous 11th century Celtic Cross stands close to the castle. It is a royal memorial commemorating Maredudd ap Edwin, who in 1033 became joint ruler with his brother of Deheubarth, the kingdom of southwest Wales. Just two years later he was killed in battle. The cross comprises two separate pieces and the inscriptions are predominantly Celtic but also reflect Scandinavian influence.

Carew Castle

Carew Cross

CAREW TIDAL MILL

This is the only tidal mill to remain intact in Wales, and it stands on the causeway which dams the 23 acre millpond. The present mill is 19th century but the site was previously occupied by a medieval building which operated in Elizabethan times. The mill's machinery was powered by water stored at flood tide and released through sluices to drive two undershot mill wheels. It continued to grind commercially until 1937 and was restored in 1972. Today it is often known as the French mill - a reference to either the architectural style of the building or the mill's grinding stones imported from France. As with Carew Castle the mill is managed by the National Park Authority. It is open to visitors throughout the season and is a popular and fascinating attraction.

for more information
tel: 01646 651782

UPTON CASTLE GROUNDS

Cosheston Nr Pembroke

Upton Castle grounds and gardens occupy a secluded wooded valley which runs down to a tributary of the Carew River. The grounds contain over 250 different species of trees and shrubs.

CRESSWELL QUAY

This is a beautiful spot for a picnic, or to enjoy a pint or Sunday lunch at the old riverside pub. The tidal Cresswell River attracts herons and a variety of other waders and brilliantly coloured kingfishers often catch the eye as they dive for prey and seek out the best perches along the banks. Across the water, high above the steep wooded slopes, buzzards soar effortlessly over the trees of Scotland Wood.

HOOK

There is much evidence here of the area's long and intensive coalmining activities, including the remains of two quays, tramways and bellshaped mines from the 17th and 18th centuries. Hook pit did not close until 1949 and in its later days was linked to the Milford Haven railway. It is a small settlement on the eastern banks of the Daugleddau, near the confluence of the Western

Carew Tidal Mill

Upton Castle Gardens

Quayside Tearooms

and Eastern Cleddau rivers. Across the river, close to Picton Point is the site from which the Picton Ferry once operated. Coal was a valuable commodity here as the mining industry thrived for a period in the 19th century and Landshipping Quay exported coal from several pits. Close by is the site of the terrible Garden Pit colliery disaster of 1844, when high tide flooded the mine and 40 lives were lost, including those of several young boys.

LAWRENNY

Lawrenny has an impressive church with a large Norman tower. Using the Site once occupied by Lawrenny Castle - an 18th century mansion now demolished - the National Park Authority did establish a picnic area. Please note however that this area has been in private ownership since 1995 and is no longer open to the public. Earlier last century, at Lawrenny House Farm, Mr. J.F. Lort-Phillips trained racehorses and put the village on the map when Kirkland won the Grand National in 1905. Another horseracing connection, nearby Coedcanlas was the birthplace of famous jockey turned best selling author Dick Francis.

LAWRENNY QUAY

Close to Lawrenny village, Lawrenny Quay is a popular area for boating which once boasted a thriving shipbuilding industry. During the Second World War, Lawrenny Quay served as a marine air base for 764 Squadron of the Fleet Air Arm. Up to 15 Walrus seaplanes could be seen moored on the river, and the officers were billeted at Lawrenny Castle.

LLANGWM

Llangwm has a long history, and is said to have been a Flemish settlement in the Middle Ages. Traditionally the main occupations of the villagers were oyster and herring fishing, with mining rising in importance in the 19th century. Llangwm is well known for its reputedly tough breed of fisherwomen, who until this century were a familiar sight on Pembrokeshire roads, carrying baskets of fish on their heads to sell in the towns. Near to Llangwm is Black Tar, a popular spot for boating and watersport enthusiasts.

MARTLETWY

A small agricultural community east of Landshipping, Martletwy is now the unlikely home of a vineyard - Cwm Deri - the only commercial vineyard in Pembrokeshire. Another product associated with Martletwy is coal, though this industry has long since vanished. Among the interesting historic buildings here is the church.

MINWEAR

A large area of the precious and ancient Minwear Wood is a designated SSSI - Site of Special Scientific Interest and in the heart of the wood is the 12th century church. Close by are the ruins of the medieval Sisters' Houses, which once accommodated pilgrims bound for the monastic community at St. Davids. Minwear Wood is close to Blackpool Mill and Canaston Bridge.

WEST WILLIAMSTON

When the limestone quarries were established here, this medieval farming hamlet was transformed into a busy quarrymen's village with smithies, inns and its own church. Today the area has reverted to farming, and is also the home of the important Oiled Bird Rescue Centre.

Lawrenny

Llangwm

Cwm Deri Vineyard

Why go by car when you can bus it!

Pam fyddech chi'n mynd yn y car pan mae'r bws ar gael ichi!

PEMBROKESHIRE - SIR BENFRO
Coastal Bus Service
Gwasanaeth Bws Arfordir

The Pembrokeshire Coastal Buses are local bus services that travel along the coast to access walks, beaches, boat trips, local villages and attractions.

They help the locals and visitors to get to the coast without having to use a car. Whatever your interest, the coastal bus services are perfect for you! You could use the service for an outward journey and walk back along the coastal path to your destination.

Catching the coastal bus is easy. They operate on a "hail and ride" basis, where it is safe to do so in rural areas. Pembrokeshire coastal bus services run up and down the National Park coastline, ensuring the entire length of coastal trail is accessible by public transport.

The coastal buses are registered local services, with fares structured accordingly. All Wales Bus Pass holders travel free!

For further information and timetables please visit your nearest Tourism Information Centre or www.pembrokeshire.gov.uk/transport.

Gwasanaethau bws lleol yw Bysiau Arfordirol Sir Benfro sy'n teithio ar hyd yr arfordir er mwyn i deithwyr allu mynd i wahanol fannau - traethau, teithiau cerdded, teithiau mewn cychod, pentrefi ac atyniadau lleol.

Maent yn cynorthwyo pobl leol ac ymwelwyr i gyrraedd yr arfordir heb orfod defnyddio'r car. Ni waeth beth yr ydych yn ymddiddori ynddo, mae'r gwasanaethau bysiau arfordirol yn berffaith ar eich cyfer! Gallech ddefnyddio'r gwasanaeth i fynd ar siwrnai mas ac yna cerdded yn ôl ar hyd llwybr yr arfordir, er mwyn cyrraedd eich man cychwyn.

Mae mynd ar fws yr arfordir yn fater rhwydd, gan eu bod yn darparu gwasanaeth 'bodio a theithio', mewn mannau lle gellir gwneud hynny'n ddiogel yng nghefn gwlad. Mae gwasanaeth bysiau arfordirol Sir Benfro'n teithio yn ôl ac ymlaen ar hyd arfordir y Parc Cenedlaethol, er mwyn sicrhau bod llwybr yr arfordir, o un pen i'r llall, o fewn cyrraedd y teithwyr sy'n mynd ar gludiant cyhoeddus.

Gwasanaethau lleol cofrestredig yw bysiau'r arfordir ac mae eu prisiau teithio wedi eu strwythuro mewn modd sy'n cyd-fynd â hynny. Bydd pawb sy'n berchen ar Docyn Bws Cymru Gyfan yn cael teithio am ddim arnynt!

I gael rhagor o wybodaeth ac amserlenni mae croeso ichi fynd i'ch Canolfan Croeso agosaf neu gallwch fwrw golwg ar www.pembrokeshire.gov.uk/transport.

Coastal Bus Network:

Poppit Rocket	Cardigan - Fishguard - SLF
Strumble Shuttle	Fishguard - St Davids - SLF
Celtic Coaster	St Davids Peninsula ♿
Puffin Shuttle	St Davids - Marloes - SLF
315	Dale to Milford Haven - SLF
Coastal Cruiser	Pembroke Peninsula - SLF
349 (SLF)	Haverfordwest - Pembroke - Tenby
351	Tenby - Saundersfoot - Amroth

Feeder Routes: ● ● ● ●

356 (SLF)	Milford Haven - Pembroke ♿
412 (SLF)	Cardigan - Haverfordwest ♿
411/413 (SLF)	Fishguard - St Davids - Haverfordwest ♿
311	Haverfordwest - Broad Haven
381 (SLF)	Haverfordwest - Narberth - Tenby ♿
430	Narberth - Cardigan

(SLF): Super Low Floor

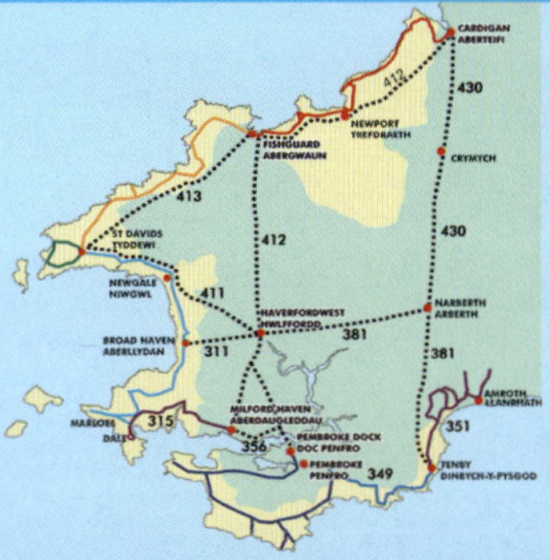

Rhwydwaith Bysiau Arfordirol:

Roced Poppit	Aberteifi - Abergwaun - SLF
Gwibiwr Strwmbl	Abergwaun - Tyddewi - SLF
Gwibiwr Celtaidd	Penrhyn Tyddewi ♿
Pâl Gwibio	Tyddewi - Marloes
315	Dale - Aberdaugleddau
Gwibfws yr Arfordir	Penrhyn Penfro ♿
349 (SLF)	Hwlffordd - Penfro - Dinbych-y-pysgod
351	Dinbych-y-pysgod - Saundersfoot - Llanrhath

Llwybrau sy'n Bwydo: ● ● ● ●

356 (SLF)	Aberdaugleddau – Penfro ♿
412 (SLF)	Aberteifi – Hwlffordd ♿
411/413 (SLF)	Abergwaun – Tyddewi – Hwlffordd ♿
311	Hwlffordd - Aberllydan
381 (SLF)	Hwlffordd - Arberth - Dinbych-y-pysgod ♿
430	Arberth – Aberteifi

(SLF): Llawr Tra Isel

www.pembrokeshire.gov.uk/transport

ISLANDS & WILDLIFE

Pembrokeshire certainly has many virtues, one of its main attractions is the outstanding natural beauty of its coastline and surrounding islands. The wildlife to be found in the area is a major reason for the large number of visitors. The islands such as Ramsey, Grassholm and Skomer are positively teeming with extraordinary wildlife, on land, in the sea and in the air.

Skomer Island

Visit a world *of* island wildlife

Enjoy the wildlife of the Pembrokeshire Islands of Skomer, Grassholm and Skokholm

Take a 15 minute boat ride to one of the best seabird and & seal experiences in Southern Britain, a world dedicated to wildlife and a perfect day out. You'll see at close quarters puffins, guillemots, razorbills, short-eared owls, Manx shearwaters, and a host of other birds. Grey seals are in evidence all year round, while their white fur coated pups can be seen from late August. Why not visit Britain's largest undisturbed prehistoric Iron Age Settlement with its hut circles, cemeteries and field systems. On Skomer you'll encounter an extravaganza of sights, sounds and smells that is truly unforgettable.

Discover the wildlife of the Pembrokeshire Islands of Grassholm, Skomer and Skokholm

Take a trip on the best seabird and wildlife experience in Britain. An exhilarating high speed Sea Safari to the islands of Skomer and Skokholm, journeying through the infamous white water of 'Jack Sound' to the Skomer Marine Nature Reserve, cruising close to the thousands of Puffins, Guillemots, Razorbills, Seals and much more.

RAMSEY ISLAND

260 hectares of fascinating island, now accessible by a regular boat service from the lifeboat slip at St. Justinian's, about three miles west of St. Davids. The island is across the infamous but spectacular Ramsey Sound, with its equally infamous and treacherous reef known as The Bitches. Ramsey was farmed until very recently. To the east, steep sheltered spring fed valleys and cliffs are covered in a wonderful tangle of rich vegetation. To the north east are sheep grazed fields. Ramsey is the only Pembrokeshire island with breeding lapwings. Chough also find Ramsey extremely attractive and both species breed and winter here in good numbers. The western coastline is rugged and spectacular with two small mountains, Carn Llundain and Carn Ysgubor, sheltering the island from the main blast of the prevailing westerly winds. The island is also home to several thousand seabirds in the season, including razorbills, kittiwakes, fulmars and guillemots. On a clear day the mountain top views are superb. To the north and east are St. Davids and the Preseli Hills. To the west, the rocks and islets of the Bishops and Clerks and the main South Bishop rock, where Manx shearwaters and storm petrels breed. To the south, the small offshore islands of Ynys Cantwr and Ynys Beri with Skomer and Midland Isle beyond them across St. Bride's Bay. The caves and beaches around Ramsey are breeding grounds for the largest population of grey seals in southwestern Britain. More than 300 seal pups are born here each season. In 1992 the Royal Society for the Protection of Birds bought Ramsey. There is now a resident warden on the island, who meets every visitor, though there are necessary restrictions on the number of people allowed on the island each day. For those lucky enough to make it, there is a reception centre, refreshments toilets and a shop. Unpaid assistant wardens can arrange to stay and help with work on the reserve.

lifeboat slip at St. Justinian's

VOYAGES OF DISCOVERY

The Ramsey Island Boat Booking Office, opposite Lloyds TSB Bank in the centre of St. Davids

Tel: 0800 854367
or
01437 721911
Email: info@ramseyisland.co.uk

If you mention Dolphins to most people they immediately think of the captive animals that perform tricks in Sea-life Parks. Tell them that you are going Whale and Dolphin watching and they assume you have to jet off to some exotic location in a far-flung corner of the globe.

Well they would be wrong; Pembrokeshire's coastal waters are home to large numbers of these enigmatic creatures and sightings of several hundred animals at a time have been recorded.

The nutrient - rich waters flowing in from the Atlantic produce a prolific ecosystem noted as a Site of Special
Scientific Interest. Here on the edge of the Celtic Deep is one of the few places in the UK where cetaceans, seals and birdlife can be found in large numbers. As well as hundreds of Common Dolphin, sightings include Minkie, Sei and Fin Whale. Bottlenose Dolphin, Orca, Rissos Dolphin, and the occasional Basking Shark.

During the winter months some of these animals can be seen off many of our headlands, where the strong tidal currents pull up nutrients from the sea bed providing food for the shoals of fish on which they feed.

For close encounters a boat trip out to deeper waters can produce some breathtaking scenes. Dolphins are a highly intelligent and very social animal and will very often seek out contact with vessels.

Typically, calves are born in early summer. A single calf is produced every 3 years or so after a gestation period of around a year. The calf suckles for 2 or more years, but starts to eat fish within 3 months and during summer months mothers with young calves have been observed in 'nursery groups' swimming along with vessels for short periods, as if introducing their calves to the correct etiquette for contact with humans. These calves will stay with their mothers for up to 5 years, learning the complex social skills needed to be part of Dolphin society.

To try to describe the emotions experienced when observing these magnificent creatures in their wild and natural state would exhaust a dictionary. The exhilaration as Dolphin bow ride, play and generally show off to their audience, leaping completely out of the water as they race along side you almost close enough to touch will leave you breathless.

Voyages of Discovery

Wildlife Voyages to the North Pembrokeshire Islands and Offshore Whale and Dolphin Expeditions

Ramsey Island Voyage A one to one and a half hour tour around the RSPB reserve. Spectacular sea caves, large colonies of grey seals, porpoises and bird colonies. Fully guided a FAMILY FAVOURITE.

North Bishops Puffin and Shearwater Voyage
An evening 1½ hour voyage to the Bishops and Clerks Puffin Isles. Excellent seal watching and thousands of migratory shearwaters and not forgetting the puffins.

Offshore Islands Whale and Dolphin Watch
First offshore to Grassholm Island, home to the second largest gannet colony in the N. Hemisphere, then a sweep of these distant waters looking for cetaceans. Last year provided excellent sightings of dolphin (over 500 seen on one voyage), porpoise, Minke whale, Orca and Fin whale.

Family, group and educational discounts - Suitable for all ages

Booking at our own friendly and dedicated office
THE RAMSEY ISLAND BOAT BOOKING OFFICE
Opposite Lloyds Bank in the centre of St. Davids
FREEPHONE 0800 854 367
Tel. 01437 721 911 www.ramseyisland.co.uk

Voyages Of Discovery have pioneered Cetacean watching off the Pembrokeshire coast for several years. A family run company with a fleet of specially built RHIB's crewed by expert conservationists, fully guided wildlife tours are run all year round. Offshore Island Voyages to the Grassholm Gannet colony and including Whale and Dolphin watching, run from the end of May to late September.

For more information call their booking office or visit the website: www.ramseyisland.co.uk

CARDIGAN ISLAND

A small island of less than 16 hectares, situated at the mouth of the River Teifi. The island is leased by The Wildlife Trust of South and West Wales, who annually census its small colonies of seabirds. The lesser black-backed gulls are the dominant species, with only a few hundred herring gulls and very small numbers of other seabirds. In 1934, when the motor vessel Herefordshire was wrecked on the northern rocks, brown rats came ashore and annihilated the islands population of puffins.There have been various attempts to reinstate both puffins and Manx shearwaters. A few have been bred but it is a long and slow process to establish healthy breeding colonies here again.

GRASSHOLM

Situated around eleven miles offshore, Grassholm is a reserve of the Royal Society for the Protection of Birds, and is the only Gannet colony in Wales. Viewed from afar the island appears to be snow covered or having a white halo, this in fact is the Gannet colony.Approximately 34,000 pairs of Gannets crowd into the tiny, waterless island to lay their single egg. The noise and sheer spectacle of vast numbers of these magnificent seabirds is something that once experienced can never be forgotten. Gannets are brilliant white in colour and dive for fish in the waters around Grassholm from heights of up to 30 metres. When one realises that a full grown Gannet is about the size of the average Christmas goose the spectacle becomes even more amazing. Writer Dr. Brian John describes the scene thus; "there can be few more beautiful sights than Gannets diving close inshore, wheeling and swooping on the bright clean wind of a Pembrokeshire summer day". The second largest Gannet colony in Britain, Grassholm is a major success story. In 1924 there were 1,000 pairs recorded on the island to an officially recorded 32,000 pairs in 2005. Although Gannets dominate the island to such a degree that even from the mainland it has been described as resembling an iced bun. Other breeding birds include small numbers of Kittiwake,

Razorbill and Shag together with Herring and Great Black-backed Gulls. From the boats that take visitors around the island there are often sightings of porpoise, basking shark and even the occasional sunfish. Plus of course a variety of birds such as Puffin or Shearwater, which may be resident on the other neighbouring islands.

SKOMER ISLAND

This is the largest of Pembrokeshire's islands, a National Nature Reserve owned by the Countryside Council for Wales but run by The Wildlife Trust of South and West Wales, who employ a permanent warden and staff. The island ferry runs from Martin's Haven on the Marloes Peninsula every day except Monday, though during bank holidays the island is open to visitors all the time. There is a charge for the boat trip and also for landing, but children under 16 are exempt from the latter. There are guided tours around Skomer, usually operated by the National Park Authority, but in the main visitors are greeted and given a brief informative talk, which includes information on where to find all of the island's interesting sights and wildlife. From then until the boats leave in the afternoon, you are free to explore via the well defined footpaths. Skomer has some very well preserved archaeological remains dating back to the early Iron Age, in the form of standing stones, hut circles, burial cairns, walls and numerous lynchets. The island was farmed until the mid 1950's, but is now grazed only by rabbits, albeit thousands of them. The flora is not rich, but the carpets of spring and early summer flowering bluebells, red campion, white sea campion and thrift are some of the most colourful in the west. The island's cliff scenery is spectacular, both scenically and for its many thousands of breeding guillemots, Razorbills, Kittiwakes and Fulmars. More than 10,000 pairs of lesser Black-backed Gulls nest in the middle of the island, the largest colony of this species in Europe. Other gulls, such as the Greater Black-backed and Herring are also well represented. Skomer, in fact, boasts the largest colony of breeding seabirds in southern Britain. This is in spite of many years farming activity during which no species of ground predators, even rats or cats, ever managed to establish themselves. Hence ground and burrow nesting sites are numerous. There are over 10,000 puffins and at least 100, 000 Manx shearwaters, the world's biggest colony. Of the ground nesting birds, there are good numbers of short-eared owls, curlews and oystercatchers, to name but a few.

The island is also home to a unique island race of bank voles, common shrews and wood mice, and on the beaches during the autumn over 150 grey seal pups are born, making this the second most important seal breeding colony in southwestern Britain. Another notable colony is that established by shags on Midland Island, a much smaller island south of Skomer. Skomer, Grassholm and Skokholm are all included in a Special Protection Area designated by a European directive, a further indication of the value of Pembrokeshre's offshore islands to international wildlife.

SKOKHOLM

This small island has been owned by the Dale Castle Estates since the 1970's and is now leased by The Wildlife Trust of South and West Wales, who employ a cook and a warden. There is full board accommodation for up to 16 people a week. Skokholm has all the richness and profusion of wildlife and beauty of Skomer, but in a smaller more gentle way. The only seabird not common to both is the Kittiwake, and in the quarry on the westerly cliffs below the lighthouse there is a colony of several thousand storm petrels, the largest colony in the Irish Sea. In 1936 the island was set up as Britain's first ever bird observatory by a group of people which included Ronald (R.M) Lockley. This of course is Lockley's Dream Island, which was occupied and farmed by him until 1940.

ST. MAGARET'S ISLAND

St. Margaret's Island and its much bigger neighbour Caldey, lay some way to the south of the county. The island has the largest colony of cormorants in Wales, located on top of its steep limestone cliffs, while other seabirds include Greater Black-backed and Herring Gulls, Guillemots, Razorbills, Kittiwakes and Fulmars on the vertical cliffs. There are very few puffins, but burrow nesting birds are restricted by the presence of rats. The island

There are limited sailings to Skokholm Island, for details contact: Wildlife Trust of South West Wales Tel: 01239 621600

Caldey Monastery

Caldey Lighthouse

and its wildlife and the coastline of Caldey are best seen from one of the pleasure boats, which run regularly from Tenby harbour between April and early Autumn, but no landings are allowed on St. Magaret's.

CALDEY ISLAND

Caldey is owned and run by the small community of Cistercian monks, who farm the island with the help of a few people in the village. A day out here is totally different from anything else you will experience in Pembrokeshire. Several boats a day take many curious visitors to this atmospheric and religious centre, and landings and access are simple compared to other islands. Leaving the boat you will walk towards the village and monastery passing Priory Beach, a beautiful, gently curving stretch of sand backed by dunes, and the island's only safe bathing beach. The easy stroll up through the trees has a distinctly Mediterranean feel to it, which is emphasied when you see the monastery. The imposing but attractive monastic buildings are all whitewashed and have terracotta roofs. The village itself has everything to offer visitors including shops and a cafe with open air seating under swaying whispering trees.

ISLAND BOAT TRIPS

CALDEY ISLAND BOAT TRIPS
frequent boat trips from Tenby Harbour
tel:
01834 844453
01834 842296

DALE SAILING COMPANY LTD.
Regular Island trips
tel:
0800 0284090
01646 603123
01646 603110

THOUSAND ISLANDS EXPEDITIONS
Land on Ramsey Island and Wildlife Boat Trips
Cross Square, St. Davids
tel:
01437
721721

VOYAGES OF DISCOVERY
The Ramsey Island Boat Booking Office, opposite Lloyds TSB Bank in the centre of St. Davids
tel:0800 854367
01437 721911

SHEARWATER SAFARIS
08081 44 55 29
boatrides.co.uk@gmail.com

Photographs courtesy of Lyndon Lomax

THE PEMBROKESHIRE MARINE CODE

www.pembrokeshiremarinecode.org.uk

THE PEMBROKESHIRE MARINE CODE

The 'Pembrokeshire Marine Code' is like the 'Countryside Code' for when you are out on the sea. It contains some really good advice on how to minimise disturbance to wildlife whilst exploring the beautiful Pembrokeshire coastline, and includes detailed maps and 'seasonal restrictions' for some of the most sensitive wildlife areas. As increasing numbers of people explore the Pembrokeshire coast by boat; from kayak to motor cruiser, the Pembrokeshire Marine Code details a set of agreed 'codes of conduct' and highlights the importance of the wildlife that inhabits areas such as the islands of Skomer, Ramsey and Caldey. It also outlines areas to be avoided at certain times of the year to allow seals, seabirds and cetaceans the space and peace they need to live, feed and rear their young. Leaflets on the Pembrokeshire Marine Code are distributed county wide, with 100% water proof leaflets available free of charge on request, and of course the information can be accessed online – just type in 'Pembrokeshire Marine Code' to Google...Marine Code Officer, Tom Luddington commented; 'We are so lucky to have great numbers of seals, dolphins and internationally important colonies of seabirds here in Pembrokeshire – the least we can do is to make sure we keep our distance, and keep noise to a minimum to help protect marine wildlife from disturbance from our activities. The code helps you to plan ahead, as many of the most important wildlife breeding sites are marked on the maps to highlight important stretches of coast to keep your distance from at sensitive times of the year...'

YMDDIRIEDOLAETH
natur
WILDLIFE TRUST
South and West Wales
De a Gorllewin Cymru

Pembrokeshire has some astounding wildlife which ranges from incredible colonies of seabirds to more secretive dormice. The county has a broad range of habitats, or places that wildlife can live. The islands are renowned, with one of the best known Wildlife Trust reserves being Skomer Island. This island is covered with puffins, Manx shearwater, razor bills and so much more. Not only this but in the spring months the island shimmers blue and pink with wild flowers. It's wilder cousin Skokholm is also a real jewel in the Irish sea, the sea bird colonies are astonishing and the beauty of the red sandstone cliffs catches the breath in the Pembrokeshire sunshine. This island also is covered in wild flowers, from bluebells to violets, the island hums with life. Both of these islands can be visited; Skomer has day visitors and overnight accommodation, whilst Skokholm only has overnight accommodation at the moment. Staying overnight allows you the amazing spectacle (or whatever the audio equivalent is) of the Manx shearwater returning to their nest burrows. These birds are what are known as pelagic birds, they spend most of their lives far out at sea hunting for food, the only time they touch land is to bring up their young.

Manx shearwaters will fly in at night uttering the most eerie calls, only a couple of hundred years ago people were convinced they were the voices of the dead making the islands a fearsome place to visit. Now they are one of the most wonderful experiences for anyone even vaguely interested in wildlife. To go on a day visit to Skomer you will need to go to Martin's Haven and purchase your tickets from Lockley Lodge. You will need to go early as tickets often sell out. Boats depart from Martin's Haven: 10am 11am and 12pm. Boats return to Martin's Haven from 3pm onwards. Another stunning island of the coast of Pembrokeshire is Grassholm, contrary to its name the island has very little grass but is instead a strident white colour. The reason for this distinctive colour, and its distinctive smell, is the vast colony of gannets which inhabit the island. As you approach thousands of these distinctive birds rise together to greet the boat, whilst you cannot land upon the island itself it is a wonderful place to visit.

The gannet itself is a fascinating bird, often seen plunging into the sea, and sometimes used by wildlife enthusiasts as a guide to see dolphins and other cetaceans. Most plunge-dives are relatively shallow, but the gannet can dive as deep as 22 meters (72 feet). It uses its wings and feet to swim deeper in pursuit of fish. It mostly feeds off fish and squid and will spend the winters out at sea. Also around the coastline of Pembrokeshire you will often see Atlantic grey and common seals, these wonderful mammals are often fairly large, and can be seen basking on the shoreline, especially in rocky coves. Please do not approach these wonderful animals but respect them and keep your distance. The Atlantic grey seal is larger than the common seals and both feed mostly on cod, squid, octopus and crustaceans. When looking out at our grey seas it can be easy to forget just what an incredible mixture of life lurks beneath that water. Cardigan Bay is home to a great abundance and diversity of marine wildlife. Throughout the year you regularly find bottlee, nose dolphins, harbour porpois- Atlantic grey seals and a variety of bird life. There are also seasonal visitors to the bay which include sunfish, basking sharks and even the illusive leatherback turtle.

Large pods of cetaceans can be seen from places such as Mwnt and New Quay, the Cardigan Bay Marine Wildlife Centre is a fantastic place to find out lots more about the wildlife beneath the waves and they will help you spot the wildlife from the quay itself.

Bottlenose dolphins are sociable animals that live in groups called pods. The size of the pod can vary significantly from several to over a hundred. This happens when several smaller pods join together to feed on an abundant food source or to socialise. They are very active and like to surf in the bow wave in front of moving boats. They are frequently seen tail slapping and leaping several metres out of the water, called 'breaching'. Females reach sexual maturity at around 11/12 yrs and give birth between April and September to a single calf.

Kingfisher

Dormouse

Porpoises differ from dolphins mainly by their shape and the smaller size of their body and dorsal fin. They are sometimes referred to as a "puffing pig" due to the noise they make when they breathe. Harbour porpoises can be difficult to observe due to their shy nature and generally only show their dorsal fin when surfacing to breathe. They are wary of boats and unlike dolphins do not bow ride. They are usually seen singly or in small groups of 2-3 animals. Females reach maturity at 3-4 years, giving birth between May and July to a single calf every 1-2 years.

Rock-pooling is something we have all done as children and what joy it brings when we find a crab, or spot a fish in some deep saliny pond. Sea anemones and shell fish give a hint at the riches which lie a bit further out, beyond most people's ability to reach, but a rock pool is a rich, vibrant wildlife experience in itself.

Now we move inland just a little, the wildlife in Pembrokeshire is so varied that it can be hard to put into words. From butterflies to wonderful woodland flowers, the cup does overflow!

WEST WILLIAMSTON

Visiting somewhere such as West Williamston gives you the opportunity to visit the Wildlife Trust reserve there, this is a stunning place with an estuary where you may see osprey, curlew and oystercatcher seeking out food, then as you walk up through the woods, past the shifting tidal creeks you may spot the extremely elusive and rare brown hairstreak butterfly, which seems to thrive here. More likely you will see gatekeeper butterflies, orchids and marsh-mallow.

Grid References O.S. Explorer map OL36 South Pembrokeshire. Site centre: SN033058

Public transport. Nearest stop at Carew Newton. Silcox Service 361 from Tenby.The reserve is situated to the west of the village of West Williamston.

Access is from the small car park [SN032059] by a public footpath across fields towards the shore of the Carew river and the south west corner of the reserve.

Puffin on Skomer

PENGELLI FOREST

Another wonderful place to see the wildlife is Pengelli Forest. This is the largest block of ancient oak woodland left in west Wales. Whilst oak dominates the woodland you will also find birch, hazel and holly.

Whilst in the woodland you may be lucky enough to spot some of the wildlife such as polecates, badgers and even signs of the rare dormouse. Eight species of bat roost and forage in this woodland which makes it a fantastically atmospheric place to visit in the evening. Common lizards and slow worms also thrive in this woodland alongside a wonderful mix of butterflies. Though rarely seen the purple hairstreak butterfly loves the oak canopy and is a spectacular creature.

Grid References O.S. Explorer map OL35 North Pembrokeshire. Main entrance: SN123396

Public transport bus number 412 Cardigan to Haverfordwest via Fishguard.

The reserve is about 2.5 km from Felindre Farchog via road and lane. Limited roadside parking is available at the entrance. There are easy walks near the entrance but no wheelchair access; elsewhere paths can be muddy and steep

TEIFI MARSHES AND THE WELSH WILDLIFE CENTRE

The tidal estuary of Cardigan itself is also a fantastic place to spot wildlife, as you head into Teifi marsh nature reserve you may be lucky enough to spot otter from one of the hides there. Head out early in the morning and spend some time in the Kingfisher hide and wait until the sleek body of this endearing mammal slides past you. You may hear an otter before you see it, did you know they whistle, keeping quiet is so important when watching wildlife as often the signs something is happening are not always visual.

As suggested by the hide's name, another fisherman is a regular visitor to the marsh. Kingfisher are often just a flash of vibrant blue and then they are gone, but if you sit long enough in the hide you may see one land on a semi submerged branch and then dive for fish. With its short tail, bright plumage and large head equipped with a long dagger-like bill the kingfisher is a striking and easily identified bird. The tail and back are a bright, iridescent blue, the wings, nape and crown are green or blue-green, the collar and throat white and the cheeks and under parts orange. The legs and the feet are a bright coral red, the eyes are relatively large and black as is the bill, except in the female where the lower mandible is mostly red.

You can also visit the cafe and shop at the Welsh Wildlife Centre when you come back from your wildlife excursions.

Grid References O.S. Explorer map 198 Cardigan & New Quay, O.S. Explorer map OL35 North Pembrokeshire. Main entrance: SN187430. Bus numbers 430 and 390 from Cardigan stop in Cilgerran village.

At the end of Cilgerran village, heading towards Cardigan, take the right turn just before the bridge, and take the long single track to the car park and visitor centre. There is also pedestrian access along the river from Cardigan.

Teifi Marshes

CASTLES & MUSEUMS

Pembrokeshire is not only rich in beautiful scenery, it also has more than its fair share of historic castles and ancient sites together with museums to suit visitors of all ages.

Carew Castle

CAREW CASTLE

Carew is one of Pembrokeshire's finest castles with a wealth of detail and atmosphere. Owned and administered by the Pembrokeshire National Park Authority, to get there take the A477 from Pembroke Dock; or the Haverfordwest to St. Clears road, then turn off the A4075.

tel: 01646 651782

see advert page 170

HAVERFORDWEST CASTLE

Haverfordwest Castle, which overlooks the town, was once used as a prison and more recently as a police station. Owned and administered by Pembrokeshire County Council. It now houses a small museum and the County Records Office.

tel: 01437 763087

LLAWHADEN CASTLE

Llawhaden is one of the Landsker castles along the Landsker Line, which is claimed to have divided North and South Pembrokeshire. It fell into disrepair in the mid 16th century after being used as a bishop's residence. Owned and administered by CADW, it can be reached via the A40 from Haverfordwest or St. Clears, then B4313

tel: 02920 500200

MANORBIER CASTLE

Manorbier Castle is where the BBC filmed part of the children's series "The Lion the Witch and the Wardrobe". Set in a stunning area, it can be reached off the A4139 five miles from Tenby.

tel: 01834 871394

see advert page 33

Manorbier Castle

CILGERRAN CASTLE

Cilgerran Castle, three miles southeast of Cardigan, is perched in a dramatic position on a high bluff above the River Teifi. Seen from the deep wooded gorge below - as it was for centuries by the coracle fishermen - it presents a spectacular sight, which inspired great landscape artists such as Turner and Richard Wilson. Equally, the views, which visitors can enjoy from its ruined towers, are magnificent. The castle, small by comparison with Pembroke and the great Norman fortresses of North Wales, is mainly 13th century but despite its apparently unassailable position, it changed hands many times between the 12th and 14th centuries. Taken from the Normans by Lord Rhys in 1164, it was recaptured in 1204 by William Marshall; used as a base by Llewllyn the Great in 1215, when he summoned a Council of all Wales at Aberystwyth; taken again by the Normans in 1223, following which the present towers were built. After a period of decline and then refortification in the 14th century, the castle was captured again for a brief period by the Welsh in 1405 during the uprising of Owain Glyndwr.

Pembroke Castle

NARBERTH CASTLE

Narberth Castle was built in the 13th Century. Its most notable Castellan being Sir Rhys ap Thomas who was given the castle by Henry VIII. By the 17th Century the castle had fallen into ruins, the remnants of which can be seen today and is now open to the public

NEVERN CASTLE

Very little remains of the castle but it provides an interesting view of the siting and layout of early medieval fortifications.

NEWPORT CASTLE

Newport Castle is another that is in private ownership and not open to the public.

PEMBROKE CASTLE

Pembroke Castle is one of the best preserved medieval castles in Wales. Open to visitors all year round, it is an intriguing place to explore. The wide walls are honeycombed with a seemingly endless system of rooms, passageways and spiralling flights of narrow stone steps; interpretative displays and information panels give a fascinating insight into the castle's origins and long history. One of the most impressive features is the distinctive round keep, which was built soon after 1200.

tel: 01646 681510
or 684585
see advert page 41

PICTON CASTLE

Picton Castle is privately owned and opened to the public six days a week. The beautifully laid out 40 acres of woodland gardens are well worth a visit. The castle lies three miles east of Haverfordwest.

tel: 01437 751326

ROCH CASTLE

Roch Castle is also a private residence. It is situated on the A487 from Haverfordwest.

Picton Castle

Castell Henllys

WISTON CASTLE

Although very little remains, the castle is worth a visit if only to see the remains of the shell keep built to help protect the motte and bailey castle. Owned by CADW, it can be reached from Haverfordwest by taking the A40 towards Carmarthen and turning off at Wiston.

tel: 01443 336000

CARREG SAMSON

Situated in the coastal village of Abercastle, Carreg Samson is a Neolithic Cromlech overlooking the picturesque fishing village. To get there follow the A487 St. Davids road from Fishguard and then the signs to Abercastle.

CASTELL HENLLYS

Castell Henllys is the site of an Iron Age Fort, which has been recreated using authentic materials and techniques. To get there take the A487 from Fishguard to Cardigan, and look for the signs.

LAMPHEY BISHOP'S PALACE

Lamphey Bishop's Palace has been acquired by CADW who have carried out careful renovation work to give visitors a rich insight into what the building looked like in a bygone age.

tel: 01443 336000

Lamphey Bishop's Palace

Narberth Castle

Castell Henllys

MILFORD HAVEN MUSEUM

The museum brings to life the fascinating story of the historic waterway and the new town's struggle to fulfil its potential. The Milford Haven story is a cycle of hopes dashed and dreams fulfilled and covers its brief period as a whaling port, which ended when gas replaced whale oil for lighting the streets of London. It also covers the town's attempts to become a great Trans-Atlantic port which floundered when the Great Western Railway terminus was built at Neyland and not Milford.

tel: 01646 694496

see advert page 84

PENRHOS COTTAGE

This is a typical North Pembrokeshire thatched cottage that has survived almost unchanged since the 19th Century. Built as an overnight cottage in about 1800 and later rebuilt in stone, Penrhos, with its original Welsh oak furniture, provides a unique opportunity to view the cottage's life in the past. The cottage is open by appointment.

For further information contact Scolton Manor Museum

tel: 01437 731328

PENTRE IFAN

Pentre Ifan is a Neolithic burial chamber dating back from around 3000BC. Administered by CADW, it can be reached via the A487 from Newport, then follow the signs for Pentre Ifan.

tel: 01443 336000

ST. DAVIDS BISHOP'S PALACE

Standing in the shadow of St. Davids Cathedral are the remains of the Bishop's Palace that was destroyed during the 16th Century. However much still remains to enable visitors to appreciate the scale of the imposing building.

tel: 01437 720517

Pentre Ifan

Bishop's Palace St. Davids

Tenby Museum

SCOLTON MANOR

A traditional Victorian country house, Scolton Manor was completed in 1842 and, until it was bought by Pembrokeshire County Council in 1972, was home to successive generations of the Higgon family. The Manor House has been sympathetically restored by the Museum Service in order to provide visitors with a taste of Victorian society and style, both above and below stairs. The 60 acres of park and woodland surrounding Scolton Manor are used as a country park.

TENBY MUSEUM & ART GALLERY

Established in 1878, this national award winning museum is set in the ruins of a medieval castle. Exhibitions of local geology, local archaeology, maritime history, natural history and a social history exhibition called "The Story of Tenby". Events programme include talks, workshops and lectures for children and adults. Museum shop with books, cards, souvenirs and giftware. The Museum and Art Galley is open throughout the year.

for all details
tel: 01834 842809

GARDENS

South West Wales enjoys some of the most beautiful gardens in the country. In this section we will take you through some of the places that are well worth a visit, offering stunning views and settings throughout Pembrokeshire, Ceredigion & Carmarthenshire, all of which are a short and easy drive away.

Picton Gardens

National Botanic Gardens

GARDENS

BRO MEIGAN GARDENS
Boncath
tel: 01239 841232

Inspirational gardens with a huge range of planting and a tearoom.

COLBY WOODLAND GARDENS
Nr Amroth
tel: 01834 811885

Eight acres of woodland garden set in a tranquil and secluded valley. Gift shop, tearooms, gallery and picnic area. Managed by The National Trust.

MANOROWEN WALLED GARDENS
Fishguard
tel: 01348 872168

Walled garden dating back to 1750. Semi-permanent exhibition of sculpture. Picnic area, teas and plants for sale.

MOORLAND COTTAGE PLANTS
Rhyd y Groes, Brynberian, Crymych
tel: 01239 891363

Small country garden with themed areas. Open for charity and with panoramic views of the Preseil Mountains.

NEWBRIDGE NURSERY
Crundale, Nr Haverfordwest
tel: 01437 731678

A small family run nursery where visitors are welcome to enjoy the adjacent gardens including a wildlife meadow, water and bog garden and a riverside walk.

PENLAN UCHAF GARDENS
Gwaun Valley, Fishguard
tel: 01348 881388

Three acres of landscaped gardens set in the beautiful Gwaun Valley.

PICTON CASTLE
Rhos, Haverfordwest
tel: 01437 751326

40 acres of woodland and walled gardens with a unique collection.unusual shrubs, wild flowers, fern walk, fernery, maze, restored dewpond and herb collection. Spring and Autumn plant sales.

PENRALLT GARDEN CENTRE

Moylegrove, Nr Cardigan
tel: 01239 881295

Set in a beautiful location overlooking the sea and coast path above Ceibwr Bay, with a large and comprehensive collection of home grown and unusual plants.

PATIO & GARDEN

Wiston, Haverfordwest
tel: 01437 751343

An extensive range of pots, statues and sundials for patio and garden.

SCOLTON MANOR

Haverfordwest
tel: 01437 731328

Victorian Manor House, Museum and award winning Visitor Centre set in 60 acres of country park and woodlands.

HILTON COURT GARDENS & CRAFTS

Roch, Haverfordwest
tel: 01437 710262

8 acres of woodland gardens, island beds and borders containing a wide variety of unusual plants. Expanses of water and ponds, wild areas, a stream and waterfalls all add to the interest of this unique garden.

Upton Castle Chapel

Hilton Court

The National Botanic Garden of Wales was the first botanic garden to open in the 21st century and the first to be created in the UK in nearly 200 years. With a collection of rare and endangered plant species from around the world, it stretches over 500 acres of beautiful, virtually pollution free countryside, across the site of a Regency parkland. Its gardens, lakes, woodlands, undulating hills and organically farmed meadows provide a harmonious blending of the natural and the cultivated. This constantly evolving young garden offers a range of year round attractions to appeal to the broadest interests. The centrepiece is the Great Glasshouse, the largest single span glasshouse in the world. Created by Lord Norman Foster, it houses a stunning display of mediterranean plants from across the globe.In 2007 a stunning Tropical House designed by John Belle was opened in the historic Double Walled Garden. The story of the evolution of flowering plants is told within the enchanting Double Walled Garden; the colourful Broadwalk is one of the longest herbaceous borders in Europe; modern water sculptures complement 200 year old water features and there are also dedicated Japanese, Marsh, Auricula, Bee, Apothecary, Wild, Genetic, Welsh Rare Plant and Slate Gardens. In our unique Edwardian Apothecaries Hall, exhibitions tell the story of the Physicians of Myddfai and Wales's unique knowledge of the links between plants and medicine. We warmly welcome visitors of all ages. Youngsters can scramble around our Adventure Play Zone and enjoy learning about plants in our exciting 360 degrees cinema. Visitors preferring a gentler pace can enjoy a buggy ride and guided tour; browse around our plant sales shop, or daydream beside the beautiful lakes. If you have access to the internet look us up on www.gardenofwales.org.uk to find out about our exciting programme of events and courses.

Gardd Fotaneg Genedlaethol Cymru

Mae'r Ardd ar agor gydol y flwyddyn ac yn cynnig diwrnod allan arbennig i'r teulu i gyd. Dewch i weld y Tŷ Gwydr un haen mwyaf yn y byd, a nifer o atyniadau eraill gan gynnwys:

- Tŷ Gwydr Mawr
- Tŷ Gwydr Trofannol Newydd
- Yr Ardd Japaneaidd
- Gardd Wenyn
- Oriel y Stablau
- Canolfan Ymwelwyr a Siop Rhoddion
- Theatr Botanica
- Planhigion i Lachau Exhibition
- Lle Chwarae i Blant
- Gwarchodfa Natur Genedlaethol Waun Las

Rydym ar agor bob dydd ac eithrio Dydd Nadilig
Haf: 10am - 6pm
Gaeaf: 10am - 4.30pm

Mae cyfleusterau cynadleddo ac arlwyo ar gael ar gyfer hyd at 400 o bobl. Addas iawn ar gyfer ymweliadau ysgol.

I gaelprisiau a rhagor o wybodaeth cysylltwch â : Gardd Fotaneg Genedlaethol Cymru, Llanarthne, Sir Gaerfyrddin SA32 8HG

National Botanic Garden of Wales

Open all year, the Garden offers a great day out for all the family. See the world's largest single span glass house and the many varied attractions including:

- Great Glasshouse
- Tropical House
- Japanese Garden
- Bee Garden
- Stables Gallery
- Gift Shop & Visitor Centre
- Theatr Botanica
- Plants for Health Exhibition
- Children's Play Area
- Waun Las National Nature Reserve

Open every day except Christmas Day
Summer: 10am - 6pm
Winter: 10am - 4.30pm

Conference and catering facilities for up to 400 people available. School visits highly recommended.

For prices and further information contact : The National Botanic Garden of Wales, Llanarthne, Carmarthenshire SA32 8HG

National Botanic Garden of Wales
Gardd Fotaneg Genedlaethol Cymru

01558 668768

www.gardenofwales.org.uk

LOTTERY FUNDED

Visit Wales National Tourism Awards 2007 - UK's favourite Lottery-funded Environment Project

ABERGLASNEY GARDENS

Aberglasney was made famous by the BBC Television series "A Garden Lost in Time" which followed its restoration. Today it is quite simply one of Wales' finest gardens - a renowned plantsman's paradise with a unique Elizabethan Cloister Garden at its heart.

A visit to Aberglasney at any time of year will not disappoint. Explore more than 10 acres of ancient gardens, wonder through walled gardens and woodlands and discover a magnificent collection of plants, many of which are rarely seen elsewhere. The fully restored Elizabethan cloister garden and parapet walk is the only remaining example in the U.K. An extensive archaeological survey carried out on the site in 1999 discovere garden features which date back t the late 16th century. Various olde artefacts were also uncovere including a silver Long Cross Penn dating from the reign of Edward c1282-1289 and a silver half groa dating back to Henry VII c1485 1509.

In 2005 the 'Ninfarium' - an indoo garden, was created within th ruinous central rooms and courtyar of the mansion at Aberglasney. Th few remaining walls were stabilize and the entire area was covere with a huge glass atrium. Th garden now contains a fantasti collection of warm temperate an sub-tropical plants includin

All photographs courtesy of *Jason Ingram Photography*

Orchids, Palms, Magnolias and Cycads. In 2006 the Ninfarium won an award for the best garden design/construction project in the UK.

The gardens and the fully restored ground floor of Aberglasney's grade II* listed mansion, opened in May 2013, offer a stunning venue for exhibitions and events, full details of which can be found at www.aberglasney.org. Complete your visit to these remarkable gardens with a visit to Aberglasney's new Tearooms – Maryellen's at Aberglasney. Enjoy a light lunch made using local ingredients picked from Aberglasney where possible or take tea on the outdoor terrace. Before leaving don't forget to visit the shop and plant sales area. The Gardens and café are open every day (except Christmas Day).

Llangathen,
Carmarthenshire.
Tel: 01558 668998
Email: info@aberglasney.org
see advert page 230

CEREDIGION & CARDIGAN BAY

Just across the Teifi estuary from Poppit Sands and St. Dogmaels is the ancient county of Cardiganshire, or Ceredigion as it is now known in Welsh. Like Pembrokeshire, it is a county with a rich and varied landscape together with a long and dramatic history and it is well known to countless holidaymakers as the home of such popular resorts as New Quay, Aberaeron and Aberystwyth. Its spectacular coastline is marked by many fine beaches

CEREDIGION

EXPLORING CEREDIGION

Historic Cardigan, which received its first Royal Charter in 1199 from King John, is an important holiday centre and thriving market town and is one of the main shopping centres for the region. Beautifully sited near the mouth of the River Teifi with some of Wales' most attractive coast and countryside right on the doorstep, its shops and narrow streets retain the town's character. The Market Hall, built in 1859 and featuring impressive stone arches, holds a general market twice weekly and a livestock market once a week. Visitor attractions include the Theatr Mwldan (housed in the same building as the Tourist Information Centre - both of which are open all year round), an indoor leisure centre, a golf club at nearby Gwbert and a large annual arts festival, Gwyl Fawr Aberteifi. Crossing the Teifi below the castle is the striking multi-arched stone bridge. Sources disagree as to whether this is the original Norman Bridge, strengthened and widened in later years, or whether it was constructed in the 17th or even 18th century. The history of Cardigan Castle raises less argument. The ruins that now remain date from 1240, and it must have been in an earlier castle that the very first National Eisteddfod - advertised, for a whole year beforehand throughout Wales, England and Scotland, was hosted by Rhys ap Gruffudd in 1176. The National

Aberystwyth

Aberaeron

Eisteddfod is now the major cultural event in the Welsh calendar, as well as being Europe's largest peripatetic cultural festival. Cardigan Castle, like so many others, was destroyed by Cromwell, and now all that remains is privately owned. More recently, Cardigan was one of Wales' most prominent ports having as many as 300 ships registered there. Shipbuilding thrived in the 19th century when the busy warehouses along the waterfront handled everything from exports of herring, corn, butter and slate to imports of limestone, salt, coal, timber for shipbuilding, and manufactured goods. Human cargo was carried too: emigrant ships sailed from Cardigan to New York in the USA and New Brunswick in Canada. This prosperous period for Cardigan was relatively short-lived. Inevitably, booming trade meant that ships were getting bigger all the time while the gradual silting of the estuary was making access to Cardigan more and more restricted. The final nail in the town's coffin as a commercial port was the coming of the railway in 1885 - but today, as a popular holiday destination, Cardigan is once again a busy centre of attention, boasting many attractions within easy reach. Several of these stand near the banks of the Teifi such as St. Dogmael's Abbey, Poppit Sands, the Welsh Wildlife Centre, Cilgerran Castle and Cenarth Falls.

Crayons and paper are provided free for children to create pictures for display in the gallery. The centre can be found 6 miles from Cardigan and 4 miles from Aberporth; follow the brown signs from the A487 at Blanannerch.

for more information ring 01239 810250 or 810882

TALYLLYN RAILWAY WHARF STATION TYWYN

The main station of the narrow gauge Talyllyn Railway is at Tywyn on the mid - wales coast. From there, the line runs inland for over seven miles to Nant Gwernol, most of the route being in Snowdonia National Park. Built in 1865 to bring slate to the coast, the Railway was taken over by the Talyllyn Railway Preservation Society in 1951, becoming the first preserved railway in the world. The railway operates on some days in February and March, daily from April 6th until November 2nd and at Christmas. All passenger trains are hauled by coal fired locomotives. Tywyn Wharf station has a shop and licensed café, as well as The Narrow Gauge Railway Museum with exhibits from over 70 railways.

Talyllyn Railway

Talyllyn Railway

Talyllyn Railway

A special section is devoted to Rev. W Awdry and his "Railway Series" of children's books, many of which were inspired by the Talyllyn where Rev. Awdry worked as a volunteer guard. Abergynolwyn has a cafe and shop and the popular Railway Adventure children's playground. At Dolgoch there are spectacular waterfalls with a tea room at the nearby Dolgoch Falls Hotel. Leaflets detailing walks from every station on the line are available, and as every round trip ticket is a Day Rover, there are lots of opportunities to explore this beautiful part of Wales.

For details of timetable and special events ring 01654 710472 or visit www.talyllyn.co.uk

CANOLFANNAU CROESO CEREDIGION
TOURIST INFORMATION CENTRES

ABERYSTWYTH TIC
Terrace Road
Aberystwyth
SY23 2AG
01970 612125
aberystwythtic@ceredigion.gov.uk

ABERAERON TIC
The Quay
Aberaeron
SA46 0BT
01545 570602
aberaerontic@ceredigion.gov.uk

CARDIGAN TIC
Theatr Mwldan
Cardigan
SA43 2JY
01239 613230
cardigantic@ceredigion.gov.uk

EASTER – SEPTEMBER

BORTH TIC
High Street
Borth
SY24 5HY
01970 871174
borthtic@ceredigion.gov.uk

NEW QUAY TIC
Church Street
New Quay
SA45 9NZ
01545 560865
NewQuayTIC@ceredigion.gov.uk

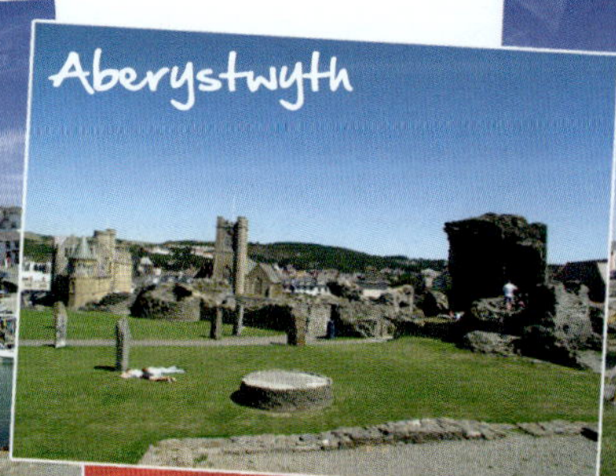

STEAM TRAIN ADVENTURES
THROUGH THE STUNNING
CAMBRIAN MOUNTAINS
THE
VALE OF RHEIDOL
RAILWAY
RHEILFFORDD
CWM
RHEIDOL
Unspoilt beautiful scenery.
Explore Wales. Discover Ceredigion.
Steam Train Adventures.
PEMBROKESHIRE GUIDE 2016
FREE GUIDE BOOK
with this voucher
Postcode:
Email:
This voucher entitles the bearer to one free guide book when details completed.
Please tick this box if you do not want to receive our newsletter.
ABERYSTWYTH TO DEVIL'S BRIDGE
WWW.RHEIDOLRAILWAY.CO.UK
TELEPHONE US: 01970 625 819 - PARK AVENUE, ABERYSTWYTH SY23 1PG
REGULAR STEAM TRAINS SERVICES RUNNING THROUGHOUT THE YEAR
@RHEIDOLRAILWAY - FB.COM/RHEIDOLRAILWAY

Darganfod
Discovering
Ceredigion
Cardigan Bay & the Cambrian Mountains
WALES • CYMRU • PAYS DE GALLES
Walk Ceredigion
www.tourism.ceredigion.gov.uk

HANES LLANDOCH

The Coach House *St Dogmaels*

The Coach House is the visitors centre of the historic St Dogmaels Abbey. The Coach House is able to facilitate functions and events on your behalf - including training sessions, workshop in all sorts of different disciplines including wood and stone carving, textiles, cookery, candlemaking, chi quong, herbal medicines and natural health and catering for lots of different functions including networking events. The Coach House is home to a number of important locally based projects. Under development is a major database of historic records, documents and photographs pertaining to St Dogmaels and the surrounding area. We are also curating exhibitions exploring social history and are actively engaged in supporting other heritage projects within the county - such as Nevern Castle. We also host the Steps to Enterprise project, a follow on to the successful SEER project. Steps to Enterprise is a support service helping to inspire,develop and support social enterprise and the regeneration of the local economy. Equipment from the centre available for hire including Marquees, Market stalls, Portable Appliance testing equipment, Ground radar equipment, chairs and tables.

We also run a thriving Local Producers Market from outside the centre every Tuesday morning between 9am and 1pm.

FACILITIES

a cafe for lunches, light snacks and regular bistro evenings with free wireless internet available

a gallery showcasing the best local art

a museum housing relics from the abbey and telling it's story

a giftshop

an IT suite and training room

a full diary of workshops, events, craft fairs and fun days

a regular local producer's market

audio guides to the abbey

The Coach House/Y Cartws
Shingrug, St Dogmaels/Llandudoch,
SA43 3DX,
www.welshabbey.org.uk

01239 615389

LOTTERY FUNDED ARIENNIR GAN Y LOTERI · heritage treftadaeth · PAVS · Llywodraeth Cymru Welsh Government · Cadw

CARMARTHENSHIRE

Carmarthenshire is a very attractive holiday destination for visitors who appreciate history, culture and a green and beautiful environment. Covering an area of 1,000 square miles, the county is a veritable feast of delights and discovery. The 50 miles of stunning coastline embrace vast stretches of safe golden sands such as the beaches of Cefn Sidan and Pendine, punctuated by the Taf and Towy estuaries, which so inspired the legendary writer Dylan Thomas.

The New Three Mariners, Laugharne

B&B, Bar Meals (from £7.50), Pizzas, Sunday Lunch, Sky Sports, Real Ales, Welsh Whisky, Live Music, Sunday Quiz Night, Bar Billiards.

All you'd ever want from a lively local!
Proud to be included in CAMRA's Good Beer Guide 2014.

01994-427-426
www.newthreemarinersinn.co.uk

Carmarthen, the reputed birthplace of Merlin - wizard and counsellor to King Arthur. The town stands eight miles inland on the River Towy - a position that inspired the Romans to make it their strategic capital. They also built an amphitheatre here, rediscovered in 1936 but not excavated until 1968. Today Carmarthen's quaint old narrow streets are full of Welsh character and tradition. There's also a first-class modern shopping centre with its many familiar high street names, which expanded with the opening of a new shopping complex with cinema in 2010. In Carmarthen you're also likely to catch more than a smattering of Welsh, as it is still widely spoken here. It is believed that the oldest manuscript in the Welsh language -

CARMARTHEN

The Black Book of Carmarthen - now in the National Library of Wales in Aberystwyth - was written in the town. A few miles west is Derllys Court Golf Club, near Bancyfelin, which has an interesting 18 hole, pay as you play, set in a beautiful location amongst rolling countryside. Another attraction virtually on Carmarthen's doorstep is the Gwili Railway at Bronwydd Arms (just off the A484) - one of Wales' last remaining standard gauge steam railways where a train takes you to a wooded riverside area deep in the valley where there is also a picnic site.

Pendine

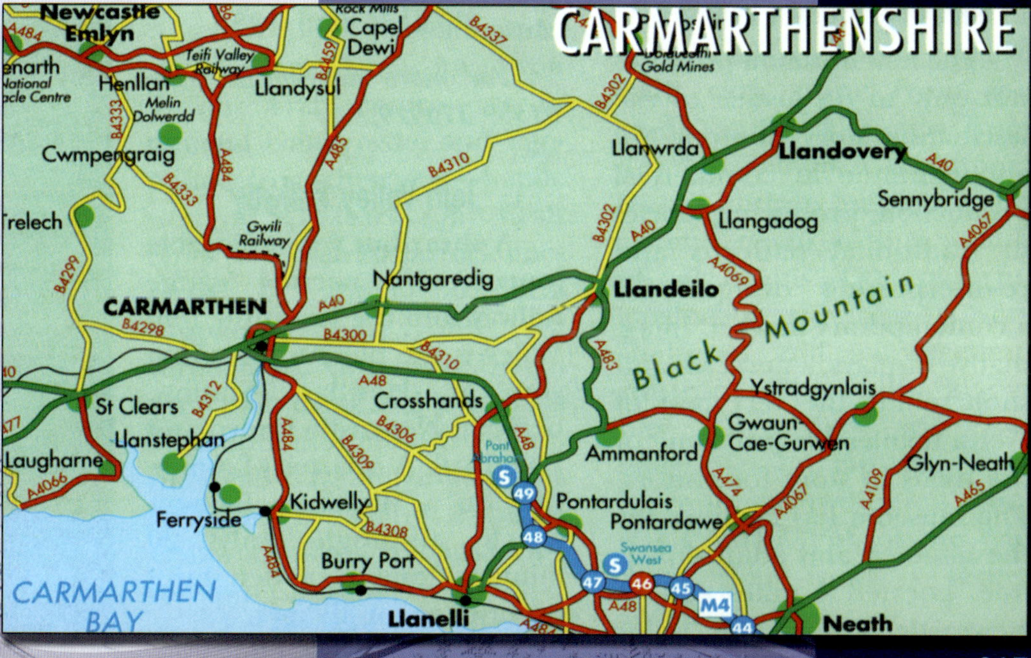

COTSWOLD outdoor | action | travel

VIYELLA

TOPMAN

EAST

Miss Selfridge

hotter®

CC

fat face

Parking for 950 cars

SAT NAV SA31 1GA

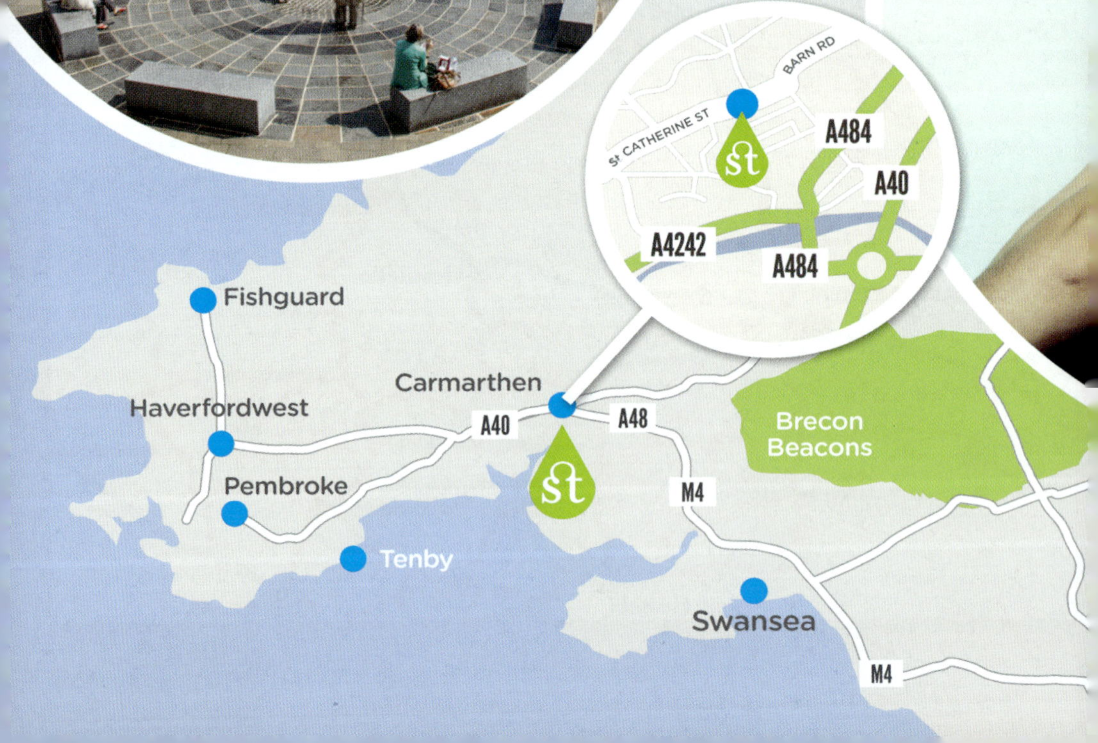

Dylan Thomas Boathouse at Laugharne

LAUGHARNE

An ancient and interesting township standing on the west bank of the Taf estuary. Originally a fortified Roman station, the township is thought to have been founded by the Princes of Dynevor prior to the Norman conquest. It has enjoyed several names over the centuries, Abercorran (at the mouth of the Corran) Tallachar, Thalacharne and modern day Laugharne. The town is dominated by the castle which was built in Norman times as part of a line of fortified garrisons along the Carmarthenshire and Pembrokeshire coast designed to keep the local inhabitants under control. It has had a varied history and played a prominent role in the Civil War when it withstood a Cromwellian siege for seven days. More recently, CADW spent twenty years carrying out sympathetic restoration work and it is now open to the public. Laugharne and Malmesbury in Wiltshire are the only towns in the UK to retain their ancient Charter, granted not by Parliament, but by Royal decree and which allows them to be governed by a Corporation in addition to the normal local government bodies.

The Corporation is headed by the Portreeve with a Foreman, a Recorder, two Common Attorneys, four Constables, a Baliff and a Jury consisting of twenty Burgesses. This august body of men meets on a monthly basis and many matters of local interest are discussed and decided upon. These sittings are held in the Town Hall where the original Charter is displayed together with many other articles of historic interest. Once every three years, the local population of Laugharne take part in the Common Walk when the boundaries of theTownship are walked and identified. This is a walk of some twenty six miles through very rough and difficult countryside and for those brave enough to take part, refreshments are served during the route. In more recent times Laugharne became the home of the famous Welsh poet Dylan Thomas and his well known work - Under Milk Wood - was undoubtedly inspired by the Township and its inhabitants. His home, The Boathouse, is now a museum to his life and works and is open to the public.

THE DYLAN THOMAS BOATHOUSE

Opening times:
May to October and Easter weekend 10am - 5.30pm (last admission 5.00pm)
November to April - 10.30am - 3.30pm (last admission 3.00pm)

Admission charges apply with concessions available. Children under 7 go free. Free admission to tearoom

Dylan Thomas Boathouse, Laugharne,
Carmarthenshire, SA33 4SD
Tel: 01994 427420,
Email: boathouse@carmarthenshire.gov.uk
www.dylanthomasboathouse.com

Dylan Thomas (1914-1953) was one of the greatest writers from Wales and a giant of 20th century literature. He was born in Swansea but his family roots were in Carmarthenshire. Laugharne in particular gave him much inspiration. Set in a cliff, overlooking the glorious, 'heron priested' Taf Estuary, the Boathouse offers a fascinating visit to Dylan's home, including memorabilia, interpretation, bookshop, a tearoom serving home-made cakes and refreshments throughout the year, and of course, the atmosphere and scenes that were used in his imagery. Built on 'stilts' his Writing Shed is literally built on the cliff and you can easily imagine the great poet here, spending his afternoons on his 'sullen craft' overlooking the hills, town and estuary.

Dylan Thomas was born in Swansea in 1914 and died in New York in 1953. He was one of the most significant writers of the twentieth century, and his work continues to resonate in the popular imagination: fans today include Bill Clinton, Jimmy Carter, Pierce Brosnan, Catherine Zeta Jones and Michael Douglas, and Mick Jagger. Best known for his poetry and for the 'play for voices', Under Milk Wood, Thomas also wrote fiction (including short stories and novels), film-scripts and various radio broadcasts. He was also a prolific letter writer and performer of other people's work.Familiar with, and in a sense, 'at home' in, West Wales from early childhood (his father's family were from Carmarthenshire), Thomas first moved to Laugharne in 1937, living in a fisherman's cottage, eros before moving to 'Sea View', and finally returning to live in 'The Boat House' at Laugharne in 1949. He lived there with his wife, Caitlin, and children, Colm, Aeronwy and Llewelyn until the time of his death.

Y Gat is situated in the heart of St. Clears in beautiful rural Carmarthenshire.

Originally a mill, then the Farmers' Co-Operative Stores, in its new guise this lovely stone building retains much of its original character and still acts as a focal point within the town.

In recent years, the building has been converted and adapted to provide an art gallery and exhibition centre, a shop selling Welsh crafts, conference/meeting rooms and artist's studios for hire, art and pottery room, café and St Clears Library.

On offer are a wide variety of facilities, events and activities, including classes and demonstrations, exhibitions and a pottery studio.

The vision for the building is that it will be a resource for both local people and for visitors to the area, providing artistic and cultural opportunities, business support and a meeting place for the community.

The Gate is an historical landmark in an ancient landscape - the town of St. Clears has a rich heritage reaching back to medieval times and beyond. Now, in the 21st century, it is hoped that the newly refurbished building will become a busy, exciting place, offering opportunities, events and new experiences to everyone who visits.

Mwyngloddiau Aur Dolaucothi
Dolaucothi Gold Mines

Canfod Aur! Dewch i chwilio am aur ym Mwyngloddiau Aur Dolaucothi
Go for Gold! Come to pan for gold at Dolaucothi Gold Mines

Profwch gyffro canfod eich trysor eich hun yn yr unig fwynglawdd Rhufeinig sy'n hysbys ym Mhrydain, darganfyddwch y gweithfeydd dan ddaear gyda'ch tywysydd a chrwydrwch drwy gynefin hardd ac amrywiol Dyffryn Cothi sy'n fyw gyda golygfeydd a synau natur.

Experience the thrill of discovering your own treasure at the only known Roman gold mine in Britain, explore the underground workings of the mine with your own guide and wander though the beautiful and diverse Cothi valley, alive with the sights and sounds of nature.

Ymddiriedolaeth Genedlaethol
National Trust
Gwerthfawr! Time well spent
www.nationaltrust.org.uk

Ar agor y ddyddiol 13 Mawrth – 31 Hydref, 11am-5pm
Open daily 13 March – 31 October, 11am-5pm
Cyswllt/ Contact: 01558 650 177 dolaucothi@nationaltrust.org.uk

PARC A CHASTELL DINEFWR, LLANDEILO
DINEFWR PARK AND CASTLE, LLANDEILO

DARGANFYDDWCH WLAD O RYM A DYLANWAD.
DISCOVER A LAND OF POWER AND INFLUENCE

Profwch ysblander Tŷ Newton ac ail-fyw bywyd Edwardaidd y gweision a'r morynion. Cewch eich hudo gan y golygfeydd o ben y castell, crwydrwch drwy'r parcdir gyda'i gyr o wartheg White Park prin a gwyliwch y plant yn rhyddhau eu hegni yn yr ardal chwarae newydd.

Experience the splendour of Newton House and re-live Edwardian life below stairs. Admire the views from the top of the castle, wander the through the sweeping parkland with its own herd of rare white park cattle and allow the children to let off steam in the new play area.

Ar agor yn ddyddiol
14 Chwefror - 31 Hydref
11am-5pm

Open daily
14 February – 31 October
11am-5pm

Ymddiriedolaeth Genedlaethol
National Trust
Gwerthfawr! Time well spent
www.nationaltrust.org.uk

CARMARTHENSHIRE

Black Mountain Centre - Heol Cwmgarw, Brynaman
SA18 1BU, brynaman.org.uk 01269 823400

Brecon Mountain Railway - Pant Station, Merthyr Tydfil
CF48 2UP, breconmountainrailway.co.uk 01685 722988

Caws Cenarth - Cenarth SA37 0LH.
cawscenarth.co.uk 01239 710432

Cwmdu Inn - Nr. Llandeilo.
cwmdu.com 01558 685088

Dolaucothi Gold Mines - Pumsaint, Llanwrda SA19 8US.
nationaltrust.org.uk 01558 650177

Ffos Las Racecourse - Pumsaint, Llanwrda SA19 8US.
ffoslasracecourse.com 01554 811092

Gower Heritage Centre - Parkmill, Gower, Swansea SA3 2EH.
gowerheritagecentre.co.uk 01792 371206

Gwili Steam Railway - Bronwydd, Carmarthen SA33 6HT.
gwili-railway.co.uk 01267 238213

Merlins Hill Centre - Alltfyrddin, Abergwili, Carmarthen
SA32 7ER, merlinshill.com 01267 237808

National Coracle Centre - Cenarth SA38 9JL.
coraclemuseum.co.uk 01239 710980

National Showcaves Centre for Wales - Abercrave, Swansea
SA9 1GJ, showcaves.co.uk 01639 730284

National Wetland Centre Wales - Llwynhendy, Llanelli
SA14 9SH, wwt.org.uk 01554 741087

Parc Y Scarlets Rugby Club - Pemberton Retail Park, Llanelli
SA14 9UZ, scarlets.co.uk 01554 783900

Pant-Glas World of Nature - Rhos, Nr Newcastle Emlyn.
pantglaswales.co.uk 0797 4569 871

Pembrey Race Circuit - Pembrey, Burry Port SA16 0HZ.
barc.net 01554 891042

Red Kite Feeding Station - Llanddeusant, Llangadog
SA19 9YG, redkiteswales.co.uk 01550 740617

Teifi Valley Railway - Henllan, Newcastle Emlyn SA44 5TD.
teifivalleyrailway.com 01559 371077

Tin Shed Experience - Montague House, Clifton Street,
Laugharne SA33 4QG.
tinshedexperience.co.uk 07970 827681

ATTRACTIONS

Cyngor Sir Gâr
Carmarthenshire County Council

Gelli Aur Country Park - Golden Grove, Carmarthen SA31 8LR
discovercarmarthenshire.com 01558 668885

Llyn Llech Owain Country Park - Gorslas, Llanelli SA14 7NF
discovercarmarthenshire.com 01269 832229

Mynydd Mawr Woodland Park - Tumble, Carmarthenshire
SA14 6HU discovercarmarthenshire.com 01269 843911

Pembrey Country Park - Pembrey, Burry Port SA16 OEJ
discovercarmarthenshire.com 01554 833913

Apollo Cinema - Unit B, St Catherine's Walk, Carmarthen
SA31 1GA apollocinemas.com 0871 220 6000

Brynaman Public Hall Cinema - Station Road, Brynamman
SA18 1SF bp-hall.co.uk 01269 823232

Crosshands Cinema - Cross Hands SA14 6SU
crosshands-cinema.co.uk 01269 844441

Lyric Theatre - King Street, Carmarthen SA31
carmarthenshiretheatres.co.uk 0845 2263509

Miners Theatre - Wind Street, Ammanford
carmarthenshiretheatres.co.uk 0845 2263510

Theatre Elli - Station Road, Llanelli
carmarthenshiretheatres.co.uk 0845 2263508

Carmarthen Castle - Carmarthen SA31 1LE
www.castlewales.com

Carreg Cennen Castle - Tir Castell Farm, Trapp, Llandeilo
SA19 6UA carregcennencastle.com 01558 822291

Dinefwr Park and Castle - Llandeilo SA19 6RT
nationaltrust.org.uk 01558 824512

Dryslwyn Castle - Dryslwyn SA32
cadw.wales.gov.uk

Garn Goch - Llandeilo, SN 690 242
breconbeacons.org

Hywel Dda Interpretive Centre - Whitland SA34 0PY
hywel-dda.co.uk 01994 240867

Kidwelly Castle - 5 Castle Street, Kidwelly SA17 5BQ
cadw.wales.gov.uk 01554 890104

Pendine

Cenarth

EXPLORING CARMARTHENSHIRE

From Laugharne, the road west cuts a picturesque route to Pendine Sands, where Sir Malcom Campbell and others made several attempts on the world landspeed record, the most recent being in 1998. The fatal crash of Parry Thomas-Jones in 1927 ended Pendine's racing career, but the exciting new Museum of Speed recalls this village resort's days of fame and glory. On the eastern side of Carmarthen Bay are the estuaries of the Gwendraeth and Loughor, and the superb seven mile beach of Cefn Sidan Sands - one of the best beaches in Britain.

WHITLAND

Whitland, which stands on the River Taf inside the Carmarthenshire border, west of St. Clears, rose in prominence as a market town in the 19th century. The coming of the railway established it as an important junction. The town's most significant place in history goes back to the 10th century, when the great Welsh king Hywel Dda (Hywel the Good) called an assembly of wise men here to draw up a unified legal code for Wales, based on the ancient tribal laws and customs already in existence. The assembly took place at Ty Gwyn ar Daf (The White House on the Taf) - Hywel Dda's hunting lodge. It is thought that the house could have been the site chosen two centuries later for Whitland Abbey. The Hywel Dda Interpretive Gardens and Centre, in the centre of the town, now commemorate this great assembly. Whitland Abbey was the first Cistercian monastery in Wales and gave rise to seven others, including Strata Florida which was founded in 1140, but unfortunately virtually nothing remains of the abbey today, its ruins standing to the north of Whitland.

Botanic Gardens

LLANELLI

Once the tinplate capital of the world and arguably the home of Welsh rugby, Llanelli is a thriving town with an impressive pedestrianised shopping centre and bustling indoor and outdoor markets. Standing on the beautiful Loughor estuary, Llanelli has a pleasant beach and is close to many major attractions. These include the recently developed Millennium Coastal Park, Pembrey Country Park, magnificent Cefn Sidan Sands, the Pembrey Motorsports Centre and Kidwelly Castle. Places to visit include Parc Howard and Sandy Water Park.

CORACLE CENTRE & MILL, CENARTH

The strange, round fishing boat, known as the coracle, has been a familiar sight on the River Teifi for centuries. It is light, manoeuvrable and ideal in shallow water, though mastering the art of coracle fishing can take years of practice. Today there are still 12 pairs licensed to fish on the Teifi, but the best place to see coracles is the National Coracle Centre which houses over 20 different types of coracle, in varying shapes and sizes, from all over the world - India, Vietnam, Tibet, Iraq and North America - as well as 9 varieties of Welsh coracle and examples from England and Scotland. An added bonus for visitors is that in the workshop you can see how coracles are made. The Coracle Centre stands on the ground floor of a 17th century flourmill, which is also open to visitors, and there are arts, crafts, souvenirs and gifts for sale.

for more information ring 01239 710980 or 710507

Cenarth

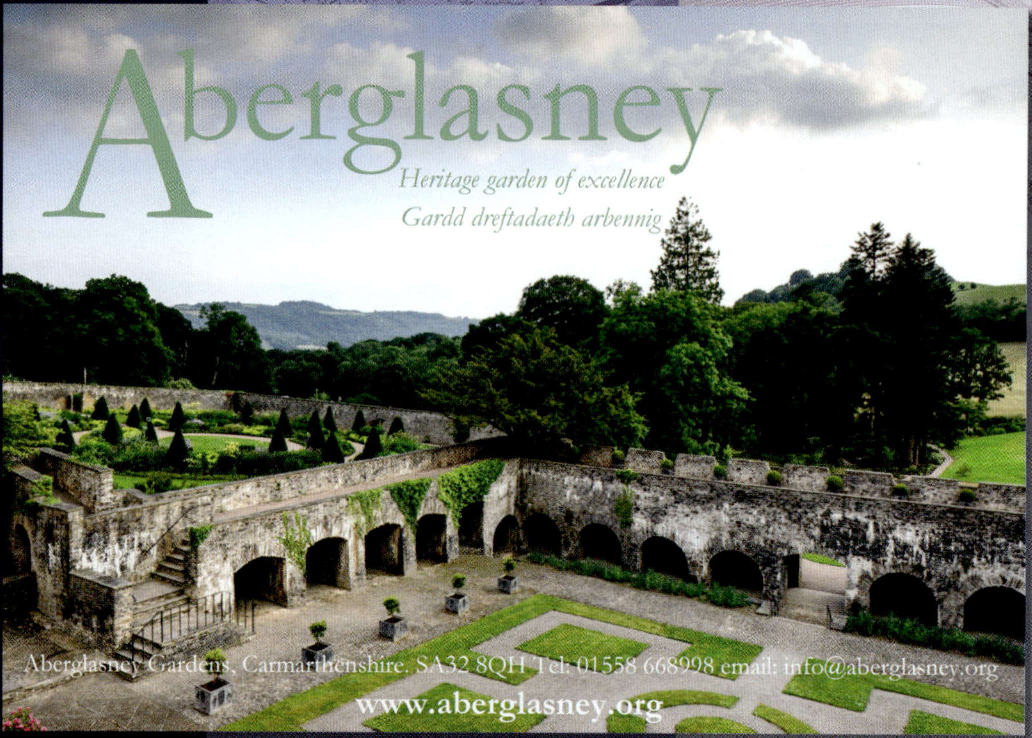

CENARTH

Cenarth is one of the most popular beauty spots in the whole of West Wales. Standing on the River Teifi, it is a very pretty village, famous for its salmon leap falls. It is also recognised as the traditional home of the Teifi coracle, and here you will find the National Coracle Centre, which despite its name is a private enterprise, though no less important or interesting for that. Unspoilt Cenarth is a designated conservation area, with many of its buildings listed. The fine old bridge is believed to be 18th century, and the flourmill, which houses the Coracle Centre dates from the 1600's.

MUSEUM OF THE WELSH WOOLLEN INDUSTRY
Drefach Velindre

Imaginative displays, a new cafe and shop selling the very best of Welsh textiles are just some of the treats in store for visitors. The museum has facilities for the disabled and admission is free. Located 4 miles east of Newcastle Emlyn, 16 miles west of Carmarthen. Follow the brown tourist signs.

For more information ring 01559 370929

Restaurant Key

LICENSED

DISABLED FRIENDLY

PARKING

FAMILY FRIENDLY

the WHERE TO EAT guide

information included within this section is provided by the restaurants in question and as such Eden Publications bear no responsibility as to accuracy

MCDONALDS (Carmarthen)

MYRTLE HILL, PENSARN, LLANGUNNOR, SA31 2NG
Tel: 01267 220861

Excellent quality food for the family in a hurry. Recently refurbished restaurant and with drive thru facility.

SEE ADVERT PAGE 224

BROWNS HOTEL & THE NEW THREE MARINERS

BROWNS HOTEL, KING ST, LAUGHARNE, CARMARTHENSHIRE SA33 4RY
THE NEW THREE MARINERS, MARKET ST, LAUGHARNE, CARMARTHEN SA33 4SA

We offer tasty home-made stone-baked pizzas and pasta, an excellent range of reasonably priced beers and spirits and cozy, well furnished guest accommodation. We have regular live music, a quiz on Wednesdays.

SEE ADVERT INSIDE FRONT COVER

SEE ADVERT PAGE 216

MCDONALDS (Swansea)

PENLLERGAER, JUNCTION 47 M4
Tel: 01792 898655

Excellent quality food for the family in a hurry, with drive thru facility.

SEE ADVERT PAGE 233

PIZZA EXPRESS
COSTA
TOBY CARVERY
Coffee#1
Frankie & Benny's
NEW YORK ITALIAN RESTAURANT & BAR
Harvester
Salad & Grill
The Real China
FASHION FOOD FILM
IN THE HEART OF CARMARTHEN
vue
6 screen cinema
st
Parking for 950 cars
Sat Nav SA31 1GA
StCatherinesWalk
StCathsWalk
St.Catherine's Walk
Rhodfa Santes Catrin
stcatherineswalk.com

STENA LINE

With a choice of fast and superferry crossings, unrivalled service and value fares, Stena Line's Fishguard - Rosslare route is the best choice for travel to the south-east and south-west of Ireland.

The luxury superferry Stena Europe is ideal for motorists wanting a rest and relaxing break, especially those with children. Alternatively between the months of May and September, holidaymakers in Pembrokeshire can spend a day in the sunny South East of Ireland by taking advantage of the hi-speed Stena Express catamaran service which travels across the Irish Sea to Rosslare in a time of just 2 hours.

For longer stays, Stena Line Holidays offers a great choice of short breaks in hotels and self catering holidays for all the family, throughout Ireland.

Just click www.stenaline.co.uk or call 08447 707070.

There are a number of facilities on board both vessels, including bars, restaurants, cabins, Stena Shopping and our exclusive Stena Plus Lounge where you can travel in style and relax in comfort.

SOUTH EAST IRELAND

Explore 10,000 years of Irish history in a day! Begin with the Irish National Heritage Park in Wexford and discover how the Irish lived from the Stone Age to the 12th century. Travel to Waterford and its fabulous Museum of Treasures, tracing the history of Ireland's most ancient city, before lunch in a centuries old pub. See how the world famous Waterford Crystal is made, then journey to the marvellous castles of Lismore and Cahir and then the magical Rock of Cashel before ending your day at Kilkenny Castle, dining at one of medieval Kilkenny's superb restaurants. A medieval fortress that has stood witness to many key moments in Irish history, a beautifully restored castle that has stood guard over a city for over 900 years... History you can touch and feel is all around in the south east region, an area linked by a network of five ancient river valleys and containing Ireland's oldest city, Waterford. Follow the trail of previous visitors, Celts, Vikings and Normans through magnificent castles and monuments, heritage museums and great country houses. Discover the creative heart of Ireland's traditional crafts and some of Europe's most beautiful gardens, cruise on Ireland's second largest river or enjoy game, sea and coarse angling in the cleaning of rivers and lakes or off miles of stunning coastline. Here's just a taste of what is in store: Follow the epic story of five generations of Kennedy's at the Ancestral Home of JF. Kennedy in Wexford. You can still see the original farmyard of the President's Great Grandfather. The John F Kennedy Arboterum in Wexford, dedicated to the memory of the late President, has over 4,000 individual species of trees from around the world. Follow the footsteps of the famine period emigrants on the Dunbrody Famine Ship in Wexford, a full scale reconstruction of a 19th famine ship. Learn the heroic tale of the 1798 rebellion in Ireland at the interactive displays at the award-winning National 1798 Visitor Centre in Wexford. Lismore Heritage Centre in Co Waterford, tells the fascinating story of the town's history from its Celtic origins onwards. Part of that story is the 17th century Lismore 13th century Hook Lighthouse in Wexford is the oldest working lighthouse in Northern Europe and now has a craft shop and restaurant.

Now fully restored to its former glory, as are its beautiful public gardens, Kilkenny Castle has stood guard over the lovely city of Kilkenny for over 900 years. Kilkenny is also known for atmospheric traditional pubs and fabulous restaurants, as well as for some of Ireland's finest craft producers. Most of these can be found at the world famous Kilkenny Design Centre, housed in the old castle stables.

County Kilkenny is also home to one of Ireland's finest monastic settlements, Jerpoint Abbey and the magical Dunmore Cave, whose underground chambers were formed over millions of years. You can also explore massive caverns at one of Europe's most famous showcaves, Mitchelstown Cave in Tipperary.

There's a mystical aura around the Rock Of Cashel in Tipperary, a spectacular settlement of medieval buildings, including a 12th century round tower, 13th century Gothic cathedral and 15th century castle. The Brú Ború Cultural Centre, adjoining it, offers a folk theatre, genealogy suite and underground theatre and an exhibition telling the story of Irish song and dance. Nearby, the Cashel Folk Village, a collection of thatched buildings recreates traditional Irish village life.

Castle Cahir, imposingly situated on a rocky island on the river Suir in Tipperary, is one of Ireland's largest and best preserved castles, with an impressive keep, tower and much of its defensive structure still intact. In Carlow, fascinating Huntingdon Castle and Gardens, rebuilt in 1625, boasts an ancient vine in its conservatory and a famous avenue of yew trees in its beautiful gardens. In Tipperary, famous Dungarvan Castle, an Anglo-Norman fortification, was built by King John in the 12th century.

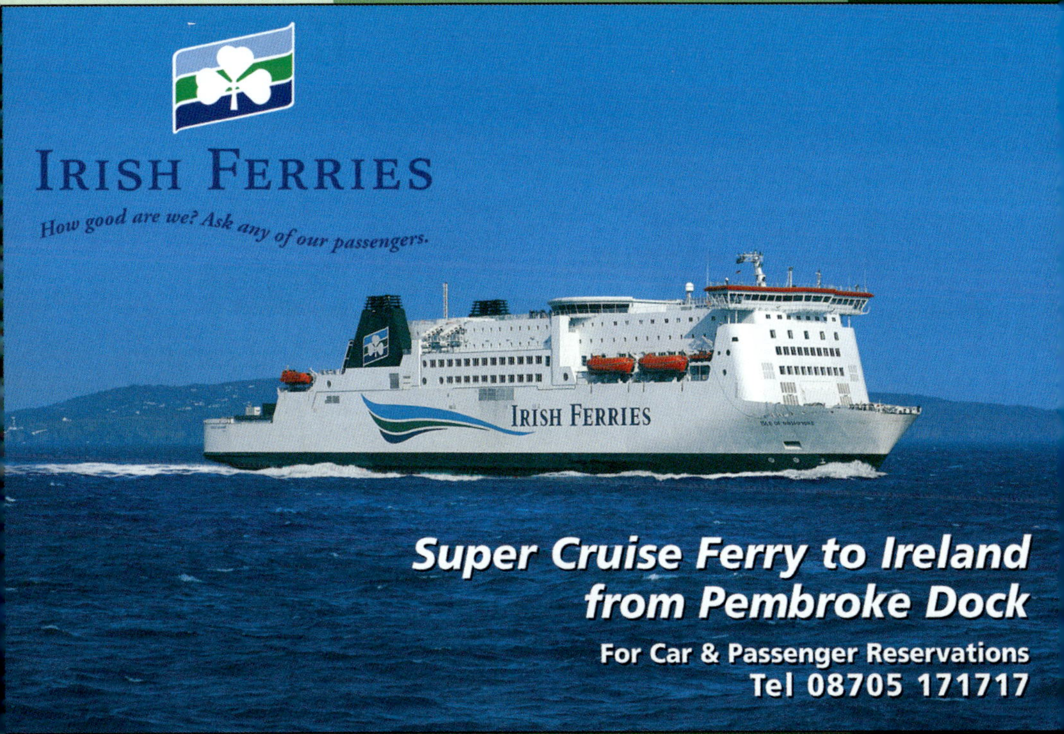

IRISH FERRIES

Irish Ferries operate to Rosslare on the south east coast of Ireland with the luxury 34,000 ton cruise ferry, the m.v Isle of Inishmore. You have the choice of afternoon or early morning sailings and the crossing takes you down the Milford Haven Waterway and out past the 2 bird sanctuary islands of Skokholm and Skomer before heading across St Georges Channel to the Tusker Rock Lighthouse which is seen approximately half an hour before arriving in Rosslare Harbour. The vessel has 2 restaurants, bars and lounges, plus a children's free cinema and a "Cyber Zone" with electronic games and entertainment. During the summer period there is a live entertainment programme onboard, also a Tourist Information Centre giving information on South Wales and South East Ireland. Throughout the year we offer low cost Day Trips for visitors to the area, and early spring or autumn moneysaving offers for passengers with cars. Irish Ferries Holidays also have a great choice of inclusive short and long break holidays in hotels, self catering and motoring holidays for all the family throughout Ireland.

INDEX

Eden Publications Ltd
3 Lords Meadow View
Pembroke, SA71 4BA
Tel/Fax: 01646 682296
Mob: 07971703599
Website: www.edenpublications.co.uk
Email: info@edenpublications.co.uk

Eden Publications Ltd are Pembrokeshire's leading publishing house, combining innovative designs with unrivalled professionalism.

Glossy A5 Guide Book, only annually produced quality retailed Book for Pembrokeshire

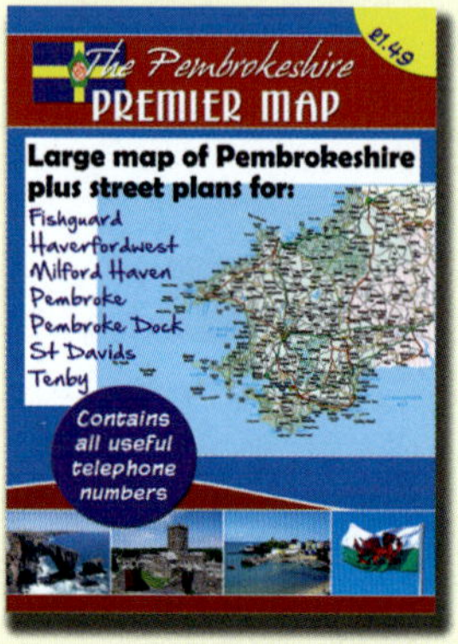

The Pembrokeshire Map, A2 folded into A5 in size, also contains street maps and all useful contact numbers

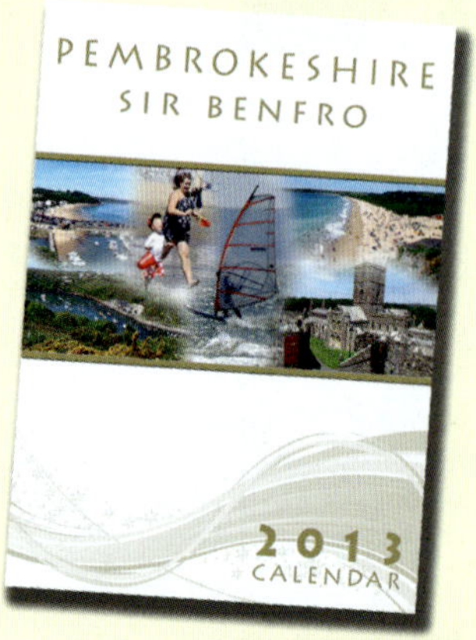

The Pembrokeshire Calendar, incorporating all new spectacular scenes

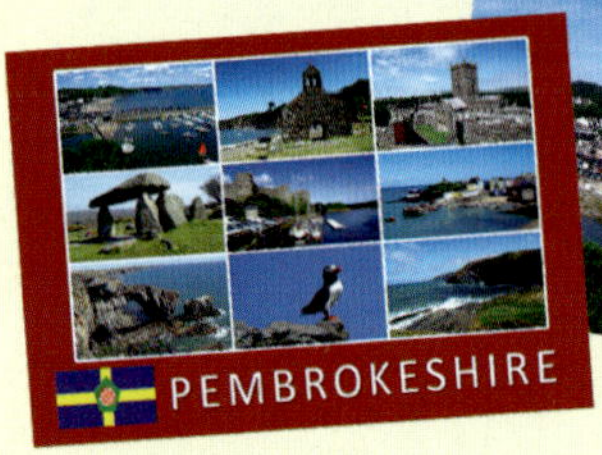

OUR EXTENSIVE POSTCARD LIBRARY COVERS PEMBROKESHIRE AND WEST WALES AND IS UPDATED EVERY YEAR WITH ALL NEW PHOTOGRAPHS AND DESIGNS

WE HAVE A LARGE IMAGE HIRE LIBRARY SHOWCASING THE VERY BEST OF PEMBROKESHIRE AVAILABLE AT COMPETITIVE RATES